W9-ADP-192

MUSKY COUNTRY

MUSKY COUNTRY

The Book Of North America's Premier Big Game Fish

WILLOW CREEK PRESS
Minocqua, Wisconsin

PHOTOGRAPHY:

Joe Bucher: pp. 16-17, 25, 40, 41, 154-155, 159.

Soc Clay: pp. 6-7, 124-125, 127, 138-139.

John Dettloff: pp. 23, 24, 34, 49, 89, 93, 99, 103, 108, 120.

Steve Heiting: pp. 2, 21, 27, 64-65, 67, 69, 74-75, 79, 80, 81, 84, 86-87, 114, 116, 118-119, 130, 132, 136-137, 142-143, 144-145, 151.

George Harrison: pp. 14, 28, 32, 37, 43, 110-111, 113, 124, 140.

Roger E. Peterson: pp. 4-5.

Charles M. Petrie: pp. 11.

Doug Stamm/ProPhoto: pp. 38, 129.

Musky Hunter magazine archives: pp. 20, 22, 44-45, 46, 50, 53, 54, 56, 60, 91, 95, 98, 106, 118.

ART:

Scott Zoellick: cover, pp. 8

© 1995 Willow Creek Press

All rights reserved. No part of this book may be reproduced or transmitted in any form by any means, electronic or mechanical, including photocopying, recording, or by any information storage and retrieval system without permission in writing from the Publisher.

Published by WILLOW CREEK PRESS, P.O. Box 147, Minocqua, WI 54548

Musky country : the book of North America's premier big game fish.
     p.   cm.
     ISBN 1-57223-035-5 (alk. paper)
     1. Muskellunge--North America. 2. Muskellunge fishing--North America.   I. Willow Creek Press.
QL638.E7M87   1995
597'.53--dc20

95-42996
CIP

Printed in the U.S.A.

CONTENTS

PROLOGUE:
THE GREAT FISH

The snow squeaked under their feet as the two shrouded hunters emerged from the cloak of the forest, leaving behind them a trail of smooth moccasin prints and the wisps of their breath. Before them lay the big lake, shimmering blue-white in the half light of dawn. They paused a moment, scanning the shoreline, and then slid onto the ice, shuffling toward the mound of brush there, just off a rocky point that nearly closed off a wide, shallow bay. The mound of brush was a small lodge they'd built yesterday, a skeleton of willow and alder, clothed in thick branches of black spruce. They built the lodge over a narrow channel that connected the deep water of the open lake with the shallow waters of the bay. The channel was a pass-through which the great predator fish that lived in the deep water would have to swim to hunt the small fish that sought refuge in the bay. The two men sought the great pale-brown predator fish — the musky. They were musky hunters.

The men worked quickly in the gray light. The young man cleared the snow off the hole they cut in the ice the day before and quickly cut through the skim ice that had formed overnight. The old man unfolded a bearskin bundle and gently caressed the alder spear inside. The points were honed sharp, hardened by fire, the whole spear tightly bound in rawhide. A single osprey feather dangled from the head of the shaft. Next to the spear, swimming in the deep fur of the bear, lay a wooden fish. Meticulously carved from white pine in the pouty-lipped shape of the lake chub, its sides had been hand-rubbed with bear grease and dyed yellow-brown over wood smoke. A final polishing with river stones left the decoy with a shiny-dimpled skin that would sparkle and flash under water, catching the eye of the great fish.

The old man next opened a small leather pouch and took out a pinch of precious tobacco. He held it up to the four directions, and then, facing the still-hidden sun, prayed to the Great Spirit, asking His help, asking that a big fish would swim to their lure, asking for patience in waiting for this fish, asking for good aim in throwing his spear, and asking for the strength to spear such a fish and carry it back to his family.

The younger man readied a bed of cedar and fir boughs and cleaned the loose ice from the hole. The old man dropped the tobacco in the water, an offer-ing to the underwater spirits, that they too would help him this day and bring a fish to his decoy. He lay down on the fragrant bed, half his body inside the small lodge, his face peering over the hole in the thick ice. He weighted the decoy with a small river stone and lowered it underwater by a thin strand of sinew. He tied the sinew to a small stick and held this in his left hand. The spear hung from the top of the lodge, directly over the hole within reach of his right hand. When he was settled in, the younger man spread the bearskin over the lodge, plunging the inside into inky blackness. Total darkness, at first, then, slowly, his eyes adjusting, a little light, a pale gray column of light that came up through the water from the lake itself. In a few moments, the old man could see the bottom of the lake, broken rocks lit-tered with aspen leaves and a few scraggly remains of the water plants that grew here in the summer. He breathed on the water to keep the ice from forming again. The light underneath grew stronger as he watched and soon he could see the bottom clearly — how it sloped away toward the darkness of the big lake, the deep water. He watched and waited.

Finally, the sun crested the horizon. He knew this by the shadows that suddenly formed on the bottom — shadows of rocks and snow drifts. He could make out individual pine needles on the bottom now, and knew that the great fish would be moving toward the shallows to hunt. He twitched the decoy and watched it swim slowly in a circle. He was careful not to stare at it, not to focus on the decoy, careful not to be mesmerized by it. A hunter had to watch for his quarry always. After a while, a few small fish swam close to the decoy and hovered beneath it. The old man smiled ... many fish make a better lure.

In the distance he heard his young companion breaking dry branches and building a fire. He thought about how good the heat of the flames would feel on his hands, and he smiled again. Outside the lodge he knew it was brilliant white now, and he could even feel the sun warming his legs through his buckskins. But inside the lodge it was cold and still and dark, and he could smell the breath of the lake, decayed and musty,

Now highly collectible with prices ranging from ten bucks to nearly $20,000, spearing decoys reflect the individuality of the carver. These three were carved by three generations of the Allen family of Lac du Flambeau, Wisconsin.

sharp in his nostrils. When he looked down in the water again the small fish were gone, and a great long shadow stretched across the bottom. The old man tensed, afraid even to move his eyes that he might reveal himself to the fish. The shadow seemed frozen in place — *was it a log?* — but he knew that it wasn't. He jigged the decoy just once, and in the tiny space of time that it took him to blink his eyes, the great fish lunged forward into full view, a huge fish, mouth open, teeth sparkling like snow crystals in moonlight, and just as quickly the fish stopped, rock solid again, frozen, and just barely, barely *not* touching the decoy.

With no hesitation, in a single smooth motion, one practiced for countless winters in countless dark lodges over countless holes in the ice, the old man rolled over on his left shoulder, reached up with his right hand, grasped the shaft of the spear and rolled back down on his chest, using the full weight of his torso to drive the spear down. His aim was true, striking the great fish just behind the gills and driving the points deep into its back. He plunged his arm into the water up to his shoulder and pinned the great fish to the bottom. For most fish, if well hit, he would simply have let go of the spear and pulled them out by the tether cord. But this fish was bigger than any he had ever speared before and he didn't know if the points or the cord would hold such a monster.

In a sudden powerful thrust, the fish lurched forward a few inches and twisted the old man over on his side. He braced himself with his left hand, and bore down on the fish with all his weight. The great fish lunged again, moving a few more inches, almost knocking the man over on his back. He was straining with every muscle of his body to hold the spear, to pin the fish. One more lunge, a few more inches and he would lose his grip. The old man, his arm buried in ice water, was losing his sense of feel. His arm ached from the strain of holding the fish down, ached from the stinging cold water. He was beginning to lose his grip, to lose his feeling of a grip anyway, and he started to wonder if he was hanging onto the spear anymore, or if he could even hang on to the tether cord.

As if to answer his question, the fish lunged a third time. The old man, his hand almost frozen now, felt a twisting pain in his shoulder as the fish moved just enough toward the deep water to free itself from the bottom. There was the slightest pause, and the old man thought just for an instant that it was over, when the final thrust came. He was instantly pulled down by the force of this giant fish, a fish that looked too big to be real, a fish that looked as big as his teenage grandson. The fish pulled his face down to the hole until the water splashed his cheek and jolted him with fear. He let go of the spear, let go of the tether cord, let go of everything to do with this monster. Never before in his life had he been afraid of a fish. Afraid that a fish might pull him through the hole and carry him back to its lair in the deep water.

Suddenly, the old man was blinded by a searing white light. His grandson, seeing the commotion, had come running across the bay to help the old man and had torn the bearskin off the lodge. He pushed the branches of the lodge aside and helped the old man to his feet. There was little that needed saying — the missing spear, the wet arm and shoulder, the marks of a struggle in the snow — all told the story. He was going to help the old man off the ice, over to the fire, when a movement caught his eye. He motioned to the old man, and they both watched in disbelief as the handle of the spear poked up out of the water, inviting someone to grab it. The old man grunted, moving quickly, with his left hand now, and grasped the shaft of the spear. In stunned silence, his grandson helped him pull up on the spear and together they found the great fish still firmly embedded in the points, dead.

It took the both of them to heave the fish out of the water and onto the ice. Nearly as long as the old man, it was the largest great fish they had ever seen, with a huge belly and long curving teeth. It was a beautiful fish, and then the young man began to laugh, and whoop with joy. A great feast would be had with this fish — for this fish. There would be meat for days to come.

Finally, the old man smiled. Yes, he thought, there would be a great celebration for this fish. Meat for days to come ... stories for years to come.

I was thrilled at the chance to write the prologue to this book, and then humbled by the task of truly honoring this magnificent animal. After all, who was I to be included in this tribute? And just how do you do justice to a creature of such status that today we use the range of its habitat to geographically define a vast portion of the Shield lands of North America as Musky Country? I am not a musky "expert," not a diehard or even accomplished musky fisherman, not a fish biologist or aquatic scientist of any kind. What I do possess, though, is an endearing and enduring respect, admiration and even awe for the great fish of the North.

As a young boy, growing up in the dairy country of south-central Wisconsin, I came to know the musky first and foremost by the many stories and tales I had read, and especially by the stories told to me by older fisherman who had been "Up North" in pursuit of the great fish. This was a ferocious creature from all accounts, savage and cunning.

My first trip "Up North," as the guest of a childhood friend at his family's cabin on the Chippewa Flowage, confirmed the stories with ample circumstantial evidence. I met the diehard musky fishing fanatics, a dedicated breed of angler that shared a bond created by the pure exhilaration of "raising" a musky, or hooking one, or — God forbid — actually catching one longer than the minimum legal size of 30 inches (a single "legal" musky was a lifetime achievement for many). I saw their tackle for the first time — felt the stiff, braided cord they called fishing line; hefted the broomstick and two-handled winch combination they called musky rods. With my finger, I gingerly tested the razor sharp points on their steel gaffs. Into my palm, I thunked the lead-weighted

clubs they used to subdue the fish. I gazed in wonder at the huge brass and steel and wood baits, adorned with gaping hooks, and, invariably, the scars of slashing teeth. I marveled at the mounted monsters that seemed to adorn every wall in every store or tavern, in every small town that dotted the northern lake country. In every boathouse of every diehard musky angler, I saw some kind of tribute to the great fish — a straightened gaff hook; a shredded landing net; a broken and splintered rod. Muskies took on a mystical air, like the Windigo, only a little more tangible.

And in spite of the overwhelming physical evidence, it was still the stories that impressed me the most. My host's uncle warned the two of us not to wear anything shiny while swimming. It might attract a musky. I didn't see the twinkle in his eye, but after seeing the abundant wreckage left behind by this fish, neither did I have reason to doubt him. Too, everyone I met seemed to have a tale to tell — the musky that ate the pet dog; the musky that attacked the bright brass tips of someone's oar; the musky that bit the wedding ring on the finger of a hapless swimmer. In no mean feat, muskies seem to comprise both legend and fact. They seemed invincible, almost, and in just about every story, the big one got away.

Perhaps no other fish in inland waters, save for the anadromous salmon, has touched, molded, shaped and supported so many diverse cultures for such a long period of time. American Indians hunted the musky for centuries, harvesting the great fish where they could, and afforded it the honor and respect due all creatures that give up their life to sustain us. Today, this relationship continues, among the Indian and non-Indian inhabitants of the North, but takes different forms. Today, we have game laws to protect the fish, and sporting associations dedicated to the survival and even expansion of musky populations and habitat. We have human industries built and dependent on the continuing presence of muskies, from fishing tackle and boating manufactures to baitshops and resorts. It is fitting that such a symbiotic relationship should grow between humans and this wild creature. In a strange way, and in spite of the fact that we do occasionally harvest these fish, we have become their friends, and they have become ours. We need muskies, their wildness, their ferocity, their unpredictability, just as they need our protection, our restraint and our benevolence.

Presented here is both a pictorial and prosaic tribute to this marvel of life on our planet — from the prehistoric origins of the species, to the minutia of its life history, to its continuing enrichment of the culture and heritage of today's North. This book is a tribute to our friend, and a tribute to those who guard our friendship.

Introduction:
Of Muskies & Men

Evil, with fins. The book that you are beginning to read is about a fish that is loved and hated everywhere it is found. This fish is at the pinnacle of the fresh water food chain and eats nearly anything it can sink its dagger-like teeth into. It is loved by the legion of anglers who devote their lives to its capture, and hated by those same men whose psyches suffer irreparable damage when they fall short of their goal.

The diet features ducks, young loons, muskrats, chipmunks, squirrels, mice and frogs, as well as a sushi menu of any fish smaller than it, including members of its own species. There have also been verified instances of this fish attacking the fingers, arms and legs of humans who dared swim in the waters where it is found.

In spite of this voracious appetite and deservedly nasty reputation, this fish is perhaps the most difficult of freshwater species to catch. The days it fasts easily outnumber those it feeds like a glutton. And when it is not feeding it has the cursed habit of following fisherman's lures to boatside but not striking, frustrating the angler by day and haunting his dreams by night.

This fish is the muskellunge, known more commonly as the musky. Those who know of the species and have spent hours, weeks, years of their lives in its pursuit will agree in the three-word description at the beginning of this chapter — evil, with fins.

The musky is long, typically olive green in color with stripes or spots on its sides. Its various color phases have inspired any number of nicknames for it — silver musky, leopard musky, tiger musky (the term, "tiger musky," is generally accepted as the name for the hybrid created by crossing a muskellunge with its cousin, the northern pike, but this moniker for purebred muskies persists) and if that isn't confusing enough, there's the final common name, the northern musky.

Built for speed, the musky is well-equipped for its attack at prey. A mouthful of large teeth protrude at a backward angle, creating a trap that few baitfish or small critters escape. Its eyes, positioned near the top of the head, are described in more than one account as "baleful." Finally, the fish is covered by a protective slime that smells, well, musky.

Muskies grow large, and the world record measured more than five feet long and weighed just four ounces shy of 70 pounds. The average musky measures about 36 inches in length and weighs about 12 pounds — a big fish, but not in the world of musky fishing. The defining size for a trophy musky is usually considered to be 30 pounds, a fish that will measure somewhere around 50 inches in length.

It is the fish that tweaks the Captain Ahab in the musky fisherman.

Success in musky fishing usually is not measured in numbers of fish caught. The capture of a single musky in a day's worth of fishing is more than reason to celebrate. Muskies have been called "the fish of 10,000 casts," but some newcomers to this sport may consider that a come-on. For the average musky fisherman, his daily success is expressed in the numbers of fish that followed his baits. If you ever hear another fisherman proclaiming, "I had a great day ... I had seven follows," you know he's a musky chaser. And you also know he didn't catch anything, but he didn't mind. There is a lot of talk of "putting your time in" and "paying your dues," which don't need any further explanation.

Pursuit of the musky has led to compulsive behavior by mankind. Serious, confirmed, committed (in both senses of the word) musky nuts have been known to forego fishing for all other species for a single-minded effort. They are the people who originated the phrases, "There are two kinds of fish. Muskies, and fish muskies eat," and "Muskies. Other fish are just bait."

Hundreds of entrepreneurs seek to capitalize on the musky obsession. There are musky rods, musky reels, musky lures, musky line, musky tackle boxes, musky nets, musky "cradles" and musky boats, which are equipped with "musky-sized livewells." Never mind that this heavy duty fishing tackle would serve equally well for other large gamefish, like stripers or catfish. Then there are musky paintings, musky magazines and musky books, which help shorebound anglers survive what some call the "trauma" of time away from their favorite musky lake while engaged in some lesser pursuit, like work. It's a vicious cycle that most musky anglers fall into when they have to work more to afford more musky rods and musky baits or buy a bigger musky boat. Finally, to help musky anglers purchase more musky gear, there are a number of musky mail order catalogs.

Naturally, musky fishermen have formed musky clubs. Are they self-help groups, organized to keep addicted anglers from ruining their marriages and lives over the pursuit of a fish? No way. Musky clubs work with their state and provincial biologists to enhance and expand their musky fisheries, using the stocking of young muskies to increase musky numbers in lakes or to introduce them into waters where muskies never before existed. Musky clubs further promote musky fishing by holding contests and tournaments, awarding trophies to the members who catch the most and biggest fish. The clubs promote the release of captured muskies, to make the fish a renewable resource in the wake of increased pressure from better-trained anglers. And the clubs are big. The national organization, Muskies, Inc., boasts some 6,000 members in dozens of chapters sprinkled throughout Musky Country. A local organization, Bill's Musky Club of Wausau, Wisconsin, founded by the late musky fanatic Bill Hoeft, has about 700 members.

The sport of musky fishing has created its own legends — the lakes, the lures and the people have all achieved almost mythical reputations. Musky waters become famous by producing numbers of large fish over the years, and many have exotic-sounding names to add to the mystique. Wisconsin — whose official state fish is the muskellunge — is perhaps the best known locale for musky fishing. Tiny northern Wisconsin towns such as Boulder Junction, which bills itself as the "Musky Capital of the World," and Hayward, "The Home of World Record Muskies," have embraced the giant fish. Annual musky festivals are huge tourist attractions, featuring parades and carnivals in addition to the fishing contests. It's often been said that after the heyday of logging passed, it was tourism dollars paid by visiting musky anglers that built the schools in northern Wisconsin.

Perhaps the Chippewa Flowage (which produced the world record, a 69-pound 11-ounce fish by Louis Spray in 1949), Lac Courte Oreilles, Trout and Lac Vieux Desert (which straddles the Wisconsin-Michigan border and is where the world record hybrid musky was caught, a 51-pound 3-ounce fish by John A. Knobla in 1919) are Wisconsin's most famous waters. Besides Vieux Desert, anglers also travel to Michigan to fish Lake St. Clair. Minnesota has Leech, Vermillion, and shares sprawling

Lake of the Woods with Ontario, Canada. Besides "The Woods," as it is affectionately known, Ontario boasts Lac Seul, Wabigoon and Eagle lakes, and Georgian Bay of Lake Huron among its top waters. The St. Lawrence River (called "The Larry" by anglers who pursue muskies there) and Lake Chautauqua are the best waters in New York, and many say they're the best anywhere.

Legendary lures get that way by fooling lots of muskies for lots of fishermen for a long time. Many of today's musky lures resemble the decoys used by Native Americans hundreds of years ago to lure muskies within reach of their spears. Art Kimball, Boulder Junction, Wisconsin, lure historian, feels the Indians tied the hookless baits to their canoe paddles. As they propelled their canoes across a lake, muskies would often follow, and a companion in the back of the canoe would then spear the fish.

Most of today's most famous baits were created years

In 1911, going on a musky fishing trip with a boat and trailer meant a horse-drawn rig on tracks to the lake.

ago and have endured because they catch fish. When Frank Suick was perfecting his Suick jerkbait in the 1940s, local anglers petitioned the governor of Wisconsin to ban the lure and its inventor from Pelican Lake, where Suick put together a string of 30 consecutive days in which he boated at least one legal-sized musky on his bait.

When he offered his lure for sale to the petitioning fishermen they dropped their effort (and who wouldn't?!). Today the Suick is perhaps the most famous of musky lures which, curiously, are often named for their inventors. Other famous plugs include the Eddie Bait and the Bobbie Bait, while the Buchertail is a bucktail spinner made by a guy named Bucher.

Either through luck or skill a handful of musky anglers achieve the status of legends. Certainly Frank Suick is one, and Louis Spray, who boated two world record muskies — and he contended it was three — is another. New York's musky-catching couples of Art and Ruth Lawton and Len and Betty Hartman racked up incredible totals of huge muskies in their primes. Though the Lawtons' own fishing records have since proven they exaggerated their record catches, and Len Hartman admitted on videotape in 1995 that he and his wife did likewise, these couples nonetheless were great fishermen.

Every locale has its own musky-chasing heroes. Usually, they are the fishing guides who bet their

Musky boats of today are often "fiberglass technoboats," with the latest in fish-catching gadgets ... but do they really catch more fish?

livelihood on their ability to put clients onto muskies. As the railroads and logging opened the northwoods to visiting sportsmen, Native Americans became the first musky guides. Today, the profession has evolved to the point where a guide must have a hefty investment in equipment before he can even take out his first client. Fiberglass technoboats — festooned with metalflake sides, weatherproof carpeting and fish-finding electronics — are the norm. In spite of the initial investment, a fishing guide has a job

with no health insurance, no pension plan, no 401(k) and no workman's compensation, with success (the capture of a legal-sized musky) occurring only every two to three days for the best of them.

Naturally, such working conditions attract characters who can best be described as colorful. Wisconsin's Porter Dean was known as "The Barefoot Guide," and fellow Badger Stater Marv Elliot is called "Bwana." No early Wisconsin guide was more famous than the father-son team of Jim and Ray Kennedy of the Minocqua area. Homer Le Blanc of Michigan made Lake St. Clair and his bait, the "Swim Whiz," famous through the application of intelligent trolling tactics.

Plenty of modern musky anglers have achieved fame in their own right. A number of the best musky guides alive call Vilas County, Wisconsin home — Joe Bucher, now host of television's "Fishing With Joe Bucher"; George Langley and Tony Rizzo. Near Hayward, young Pete

Maina put together an incredible string of more than 200 legal-sized muskies per year for himself and his clients for several years running.

In Minnesota, the musky-catching duo of Dick and Betty Pearson are well known, as is Lake of the Woods musky stalker Doug Johnson. Of course, the *In-Fisherman* magazine crew boasts some great musky fishermen, most notably Al Lindner and Doug Stange. Steve Herbeck, formerly one of Wisconsin's best-ever, now runs a fishing camp on Ontario's Eagle Lake. Another legend from Ontario, Don Pursch, specializes in the clear water of Rowan Lake. A magazine article called New Yorker Al Russell the "best musky guide on the St. Lawrence River," and a great St. Lawrence fisherman and guide whose catches and fame have stood the test of time is Jim Evans.

The sport has also attained celebrity status. General Dwight Eisenhower frequently traveled to northern Wisconsin to battle muskies. A well-known picture dated July 17, 1946 shows the future United States president and his four brothers with five muskies they caught from Pine Lake in Iron County, Wisconsin. A photo housed in the archives of the Wisconsin State Historical Society and dated September 25, 1937, pictures Wisconsin Governor Robert LaFollette, Illinois Governor Henry Horner and Iowa

Arthur, Dwight, Edgar, Milton and Earl Eisenhower with five muskies and a northern pike they caught on Pine Lake, Iron County, Wisconsin, on July 17, 1946. At right, a priceless color photo of Gypsy Rose Lee with a big tiger musky caught from a Vilas County, Wisconsin, lake in October 1968. Comparing the happiness on her face to the expression of the boat's rower, Gypsy reveals it's much more fun to be the "catcher" of the musky.

Governor Nels G. Kraschel with a catch of muskellunge. General Jimmy Doolittle, who led the daring bomber attack over Tokyo less than five months after the Japanese attack on Pearl Harbor and who was later honored with the Congressional Medal of Honor, was known to frequent Tomahawk Lake in Oneida County, Wisconsin.

Everyone knows of actress Elizabeth Taylor, but few know that she spent her childhood summers in Minocqua, Wisconsin. Though she preferred to fish for bass, she also caught a few muskies. Once she caught a 29-inch musky (30 inches was the legal minimum back then), and according to the late guide, Ed Behrend, in a magazine article, "it broke her heart to throw

Famous newsman Edward R. Murrow slugs it out with a Vilas County, Wisconsin, musky in 1957. With him are Wisconsin Conservation Department officials Arthur A. Oehmcke (on the oars) and Art MacArthur. At right, baseball legend Ted Williams with a 21-pound musky from South Twin Lake, Vilas County, Wisconsin, in 1948.

it back." Gypsy Rose Lee was a frequent client of Porter Dean, while Jane Russell and Janet Gaynor also are reported to have enjoyed musky fishing. Famous newsman Edward R. Murrow caught a musky while fishing with Wisconsin Conservation Department officials. Baseball Hall of Famer Ted Williams loved his musky fishing as did National Football League Hall of Famer Forrest Gregg. Lately, rock star Frankie Sullivan, of the group "Survivor," has earned a solid reputation for his musky exploits.

Some musky fishermen were notorious for other reasons. Northern Wisconsin was the hideout for Chicago's mobsters during the 1930s, adding another twist to the musky story. When things got too hot in Chicago, a number of the more famous crime bosses spent time "on the lam," waiting for things to "cool off" in Chicago. With plenty of spare time, they often went musky fishing.

Legendary conservation warden Ernie Swift, who later became director of the Wisconsin Conservation Department, seemed to be constantly chasing gangsters near the Winter Dam in Sawyer County during the 1930s — the confrontations ended with verbal showdowns that never quite made it to gun battle — with Ernie winning. Among the mobsters Swift encountered were "Machine Gun Frankie" MacErlane and "Beer Baron" Joe Saltis, while warden H. B. "Happy" Haugan slugged it out with "Lefty" Koncel.

Rock star Frankie Sullivan, of the group "Survivor," has become an avid and expert musky angler.

The gangster influence in northern Wisconsin even resulted in a rumor that Louis Spray bought his world record musky from a fugitive on the lam. However, exhaustive research by musky historian John Dettloff proved conclusively that Spray indeed caught his fish.

Today, the one-time presence of the mobsters is still felt. The Little Bohemia Resort in Vilas County, the site of a late-night shootout between law agents and John Dillinger and his gang, is a popular tourist attraction. Near Hayward, Al Capone's encampment is preserved today as "The Hideout," and remains complete with gun turret.

So far you have been introduced to what the musky mystique is and how it has grabbed the rich, the poor and the famous. What we have yet to investigate is why fishermen become enthralled with musky fishing. People who do not understand what musky fishing is all about are confused by the antics of the musky fisherman. Musky fishing is much more than the idea of chasing the will-o'-the-wisp.

There is something that lures musky hunters back to their favorite lakes that goes beyond the capture of a musky. It could be that muskies are typically found in some of the most beautiful country North America has to offer. The scent of white pines on a far northern lake and the sound of the wind whispering through them is certainly part of it. There is the haunting cry of the common loon on a summer's evening, the whistling of duck wings and the calls of migrating Canada geese in fall, the wonderment of a Canadian Shield lake's vertical rock walls, the awe of a thunderstorm building on the horizon, the sting of snow on your face during the days just before the lake freezes over.

The country that muskies are found in is symbolic of the fish itself — wild, beautiful, inspirational. It is difficult to capture this land in words, just as it is difficult to capture the musky. Just when you think you have attained your goal it escapes you, like the football halfback who gives you a leg before he takes it away, like the lightly-hooked musky that thrashes free at boatside.

Perhaps that is why people fish for muskies — to attempt to touch, if just for a moment, something that is wild and knows no rules. Perhaps this is a primeval desire, a throwback to the day when a man's worth was measured by his ability to kill animals to feed his family or clan. The urge bridges generation gaps and social classes. It enthralls fishermen, no matter if they are a 12-year-old kid wearing air conditioned tennis shoes or a Hollywood starlet.

The muskellunge may indeed be "evil, with fins," but the pursuit of the fish is an experience in itself, a big adventure, and therefore good for the soul of the angler.

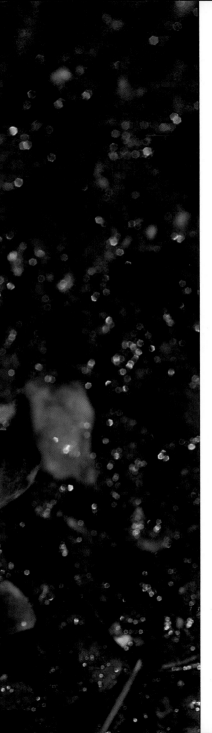

EVOLUTION AND NATURAL HISTORY

I t is very difficult to talk about the muskellunge without mention of the fishes to which it is related. One of the fascinations of nature is that this fish, which can exceed 60 pounds of weight, belongs to a worldwide group of 12 species including several that do not exceed four inches length and a few ounces weight. In fact, many people are unaware of the relationship of the larger and smaller species. As presently organized, the families *Esocidae* (muskellunge, pikes and pickerels) and *Umbridae* (mudminnows and blackfishes) comprise the group. Esocidae includes the muskellunge, *Esox masquinongy*, the pike, *Esox lucius*, the Amur pike, *Esox reicherti*, the chain pickerel, *Esox niger*, and the grass and redfin pickerels, *Esox americanus*. *Umbridae* includes the more diminutive species — the European mudminnow, *Umbra krameri*, the eastern mudminnow, *Umbra pygmaea*, central mudminnow, *Umbra limi*, Olympic mudminnow, *Novumbra hubbsi*, and the Alaska blackfish, *Dallia pectoralis*, plus the two Siberian blackfishes, *Dallia delicatissima* and *Dallia admirabilis*.

The difference in distribution are also of interest. The pike occurs around the world in the Northern Hemisphere, the Amur pike is limited to a single river system, the Amur or Heilungjiang River, which, for much of its length, is the border between China and Russia. The present, natural range of the muskellunge and the three pickerels is eastern North America. One mudminnow occurs only in central Europe, the next two in eastern North America, and the Olympic mudminnow is restricted to a small portion of the state of Washington. The blackfishes occur only on the two sides of the Pacific Ocean, the first in Alaska and the eastern tip of Siberia, the other two only on the tip of Siberia. Many of these points have interesting implications in regard to the origins and subsequent dispersal of the various species or groups of species.

This variation in size, distribution and external appearance has been one of the problems in attempts to clarify the relationships within the group, and that of this group to other groups of fishes. Over the years the position of the pikes and mudminnows in the genealogy of all fishes has shifted considerably. At one time they were thought to be a fairly advanced group, then less advanced and related to the herrings or the salmons and trouts. At present they are placed on the tree as a unit basal to all the other true bony fishes. This confusion is reflected in the fact that even today this group of fishes is assigned, by various authors, to a "superorder" *Esocae*, to the suborder *Esocoidei* of the dismantled order of salmon, trouts etc., or to a separate order *Esociformes*.

When the fossil history of the group was less well known than at present, and the concept of continental drift was unknown, it was thought that the *esocoid* fishes arose in southeast Germany and spread to North America. The putative ancestral form was a now extinct mudminnow *Palaeoesox fritschei* which lived about 40 million years ago. Very recent fossil discoveries in Canada, made by paleontologists at the University of Edmonton, first pushed the history back to 62 million years ago with a species, *Esox tiemani*, which was very like modern pikes and may be the ancestral form. More recent fossil discoveries, in Montana, Wyoming and Alberta, by the same scientists, revealed that several species of pikes occurred in North America at least 70 million years ago, at a time when North America and Eurasia were still joined and a seaway virtually divided "North America" into separate eastern and western continents. Those discoveries suggest that pikes and mudminnows could have arisen on the combined North America-Eurasia land mass and diversified in both areas.

In regard to the muskellunge alone, fossil records

are limited to North America and suggest that the musky existed at least 2 million to 10 million years ago. The other interesting fact about those fossils is that they were found in Washington and Oregon, and if they do represent this species they would indicate that it must have occurred over a much broader area in the past than it does today. This ties in with the idea that the Olympic mudminnow is a relict of a once much more widely distributed fauna. Another indication of a broader distribution is fossils attributed to the muskellunge which were found in Oklahoma, Kansas and Michigan. Those date from 0.5 million years to 14,000 years ago, from the interglacial period to the end of the last glacier. There are many more fossils identified only as *Esox*, which could be the muskellunge or another species. Those are not included here.

It would appear then that the muskellunge evolved in North America sometime prior to 10 million years ago, possibly from *Esox tiemani*, or some other undiscovered ancestral form. Since that time it has undergone certain changes in response to changes in environment, available habitats, and isolation in separate groups in different locations for varying periods of time. It has, however, retained what must be considered a set of very old general family characteristics (e.g. position of the unpaired fins; well-toothed, protracted snout; body shape) which is

probably as old as 60 million years.

How many kinds of muskellunge are there? The answer to that question has to take into consideration origin, evolution, recent history (postglacial), the history of human understanding of the distinction between animal forms referred to as species, and the factors involved in their change over time. The muskellunge was recognized as a distinct species only around 1820 and was formally described by a New York medical doctor, Samuel Latham Mitchill, in 1824 in a magazine- or newspaper-type periodical referred to later as *The Mirror*. The description is said to have been based on a specimen from Lake Erie. Sadly enough, no copy of the publication has been seen since the mid 1800s, in spite of diligent searches by a number of ichthyologists including this author. Prior to that and for some time after, there was considerable confusion between the pike and muskellunge. Both common and scientific names were used interchangeably for some time.

As anglers and people interested in natural history moved west, and communication between such people improved, it was discovered that there were three forms of muskellunge-like fish with different patterns. Eventually these three forms were described as separate species. *Esox masquinongy* from the Great Lakes, with a spotted pattern, retained Mitchill's

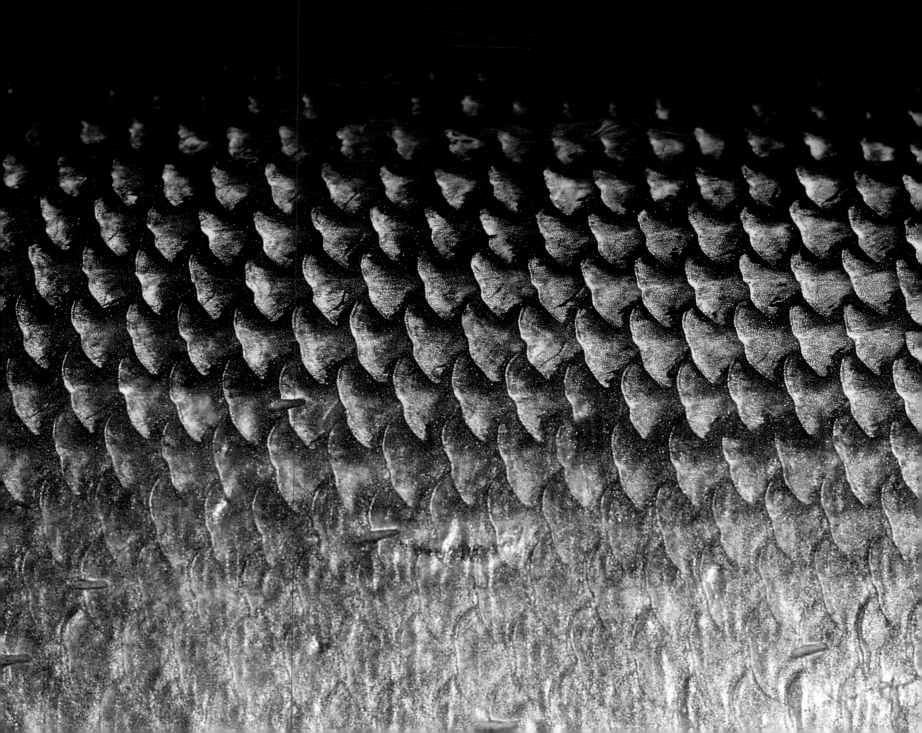

original name. Muskellunge in the Ohio River system, including headwater Chautauqua Lake in New York, with prominent bars became *Esox ohioensis*. Individuals in Wisconsin and Minnesota (and by extension northwestern Ontario), with little lateral pattern or diffuse bars or blotches, became *Esox immaculatus*.

Although you will still see these names in the literature, as time passed and more was learned about the muskellunge the concept was adopted of three races of a single species, *Esox masquinongy*. Although there were obvious differences they appeared to be more environmentally than genetically based. In spite of regional differences in adult pattern, all young-of-the-year muskellunge, regardless of regional origin, start out with the same color pattern. The parallel was the retention of a single species and scientific name for three life history forms of rainbow trout — rainbow, Kamloops and steelhead.

Several factors strongly indicate that during the last glacial period the muskellunge existed south of the glacier in some part(s) of the present Mississippi River system. Its present distribution, particularly in the northern areas long covered by the glacier, indicates that it followed a number of postglacial pathways, reaching present areas as much as 7,000 years later than others. That could have provided the isolation and opportunity for the development of differences.

More recently there has been a suggestion of the existence of two species without discrete geographical separation. In this line of thinking, the presently-recognized species would be limited to bodies of water in which pike and muskellunge occur together (e.g. the Great Lakes) and would be called the "riverine species," and a new species would be recognized in those waters throughout the area of distribution in which the muskellunge occurs alone (e.g. the Kawartha Lakes of Ontario), called the "lacustrine species." This concept has not met with wide agreement nor, to my knowledge, has it been published. For simplicity it will be assumed here that there is only one variable species.

The hybrid between the pike and the muskellunge, which occurs naturally in waters occupied by both parent species, is now almost universally known as tiger muskellunge, tiger musky, or tiger. One must be cautious using older literature since the word "tiger" was often used for individual muskellunge anywhere with prominent stripes. The male of this form is virtually totally sterile as is typical of hybrids. There is some limited fertility in some females. The hybrid is now cultured widely and has been introduced into waters within and beyond the natural distribution of the muskellunge. It has long been known in the wild, but created confusion when a scientific

name, *Esox amentus*, appeared in the popular literature. A 1948 study in Ontario finally identified this form for what it was. One indicator of the low level of reproductive isolation of species in this family of fishes is the fact that hybrids can be developed combining even the largest and smallest species in the family.

Another interesting form, which is actually a special morph of the pike, must be mentioned in passing. This is the so-called silver pike which is distinguishable from other individuals only by the absence of the typical spotted pattern of the pike, the overall silver-blue coloration, and an apparent greater tenacity for life. It was first described from Sharbot Lake, Ontario, in 1897. It is mentioned here because it was once thought to be a kind of muskellunge ("silver muskellunge") and was cultured along with muskellunge and released in lakes near Nevis, Minnesota, in the 1930s.

Extensive information on means of distinguishing between the muskellunge, the pike, and the tiger muskellunge is available in the book *Managing Muskies*, produced by the American Fisheries Society.

The coloration of the hybrid, or "tiger" musky, is well illustrated by this fish, caught Aug. 14, 1992 from Sand Lake in Vilas County, Wisconsin by Corey Meyer. The musky is the catch and release world record in the "unlimited" line class.

That includes new information on the use of characteristics of scales, cleithrum bone, spinal column, individual vertebra, and teeth.

The natural distribution of the muskellunge has undergone several waves of expansion and contraction over time. Most recently these have involved reductions resulting from deterioration of habitats south of the Great Lakes and introductions beyond the natural range by fish culture. In many places within what might be thought of as the natural range of the species, populations are maintained only by irregular or constant hatchery support.

The present eastern limit of occurrence is the central portion of the St. John River of New Brunswick. The population in that unusual location results from natural downstream dispersal after introductions in Quebec north of New Brunswick. The distribution extends into southern Quebec, including the Ottawa River and much of the Eastern Townships, south in the Lake Champlain portion of Vermont, western New York peripheral to the Great Lakes, Chautauqua Lake and other parts of the Ohio River system in that state, and introduced into other areas including the Susquehanna River system. New Jersey, once outside the range, now has introduced populations in the Delaware River. Once native to only extreme northwestern Pennsylvania it has been introduced into a number of locations around the state. One of these is the Youghiogheny Reservoir shared with Maryland so the species may be in that state as well. In Virginia it occurs in the western uplands and in scattered locations near the coast as a result of introductions begun in 1963. It also occurs in West Virginia, most of eastern and south-central Kentucky, eastern Tennessee, is native to the French Broad and Little Tennessee rivers in extreme western North Carolina, and has been introduced into reservoirs elsewhere in that state. This species was also introduced in the Tennessee River system of extreme northern Georgia. Muskellunge were stocked in Norfolk and Gray reservoirs in Arkansas but never became established. This species has been introduced into central Missouri, starting in 1966.

Although native to northern Illinois it was apparently never common there, is said to have been largely extirpated and then reinstated by introductions into many reservoirs. It is sparsely distributed in northern Indiana, and now general throughout Ohio, but away from the Ohio River system the populations are supported by stocking. In Iowa there were records of its existence in the Mississippi River up to 1945, the population diminished or disappeared and the species was reintroduced starting in 1960 into the Okoboji lakes chain in northwestern Iowa. In 1972 it was said that muskellunge had a very limited occurrence in north-central Nebraska. In Michigan the species is peripheral to the Great Lakes and in the Upper Peninsula in the area of the border with Wisconsin. In Wisconsin naturally-reproducing populations are mainly confined to the northern and western sections, the Mississippi system only to Lake Pepin, and the border with Michigan. Populations farther south are maintained by stocking. In Minnesota the species occurs in parts of the systems of the Mississippi and St. Croix rivers, in the Rainy River area, and scattered lakes elsewhere.

This western segment of the species continues north into northwestern Ontario west of Rainy Lake in the systems of both the Winnipeg and English rivers, Lake of the Woods and westward into Manitoba were the populations in the western part of the province have been established by introductions. In Ontario there is an isolated population in the Pic River, tributary to the north shore of Lake Superior, but the eastern portion of the distribution is largely below a line from Sault Ste. Marie to the Ottawa River and south throughout southern Ontario including the lower Great Lakes and St. Lawrence River. This species was introduced into North

One of the side benefits to musky fishing is the sheer beauty of many of the lakes in which it is found.

Dakota in 1958 and occurs in parts of the systems of both the Missouri and Red river systems, as well as in several lakes throughout the state. Ohio muskellunge were stocked in South Dakota, starting in 1979, in pits and ponds and the reservoir of the Big Stone Power Plant. It was also introduced into Arizona about 1973, into a closed basin lake near Flagstaff.

Older, unsuccessful attempts to introduce the species more widely include Lake Merced, California, in 1893, Cape Cod in 1854, and possibly New Hampshire in 1838.

The hybrid between the muskellunge and the pike, usually called tiger muskellunge, has been widely cultured and introduced. It is usually introduced in locations beyond the present "natural range" of the muskellunge. Possibly the most recent successful use of this form (a hybrid is not referred to as a species) that has gained notoriety was its introduction into reservoir waters east of Denver, Colorado. A survey of the literature indicated that the hybrid has been introduced in at least the following areas: Arkansas, Colorado, Illinois, Indiana, Iowa, Michigan, Minnesota, Missouri, Montana, New Jersey, New York, North Carolina, Ohio, Pennsylvania, Vermont, Virginia, Washington and Wisconsin. As indicated in a previous section this hybrid appears in nature also, probably as a result of a late-spawning pike and an early-spawning muskellunge using the same spawning ground. Some lakes seem to develop an unusually high number of hybrids (e.g. Lac Vieux Desert, Michigan-Wisconsin, and Dalrymple Lake, Ontario).

For simplicity, the life history of the muskellunge will be presented here as that of a single, but variable, species. Other than at spawning time this species can be said to be a solitary, sedentary animal, usually found in the shallow to moderately deep water of flowing or standing temperate habitats characterized by the presence of lush growths of emergent and non-emergent aquatic vegetation and cover in the form of stumps and fallen trees. In its native range the community of fishes usually includes species of suckers, catfishes, perches, sunfishes and a number of minnows.

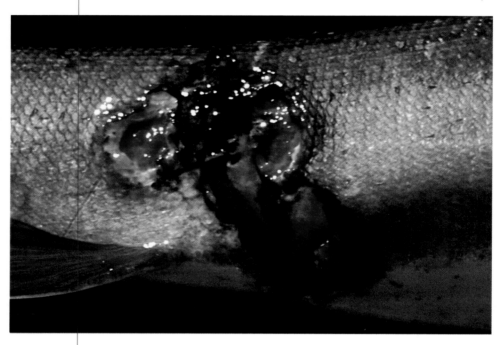

Lymphocarcoma is an ugly, but not necessarily fatal, disease that muskies occasionally suffer from. It is often spread during spawning.

Much has been learned, at least for adults, about the way individuals use their habitat. They have home ranges, sometimes different ranges depending on season, and they have movement patterns in different seasons that are cued by, and predictable on, the basis of habitat conditions. Nature and extent of directed and "random" movements depend on the nature (lake or river) and size of the habitat.

Muskellunge first attain reproductive capacity between four and six years of age depending on locality and sex; females maturing later and at greater size. Spawning takes place in the spring immediately following, or overlapping, spawning by pike. Spawners home to specific spawning sites and spawn in that vicinity several years in succession. The nature of the spawning site (current, depth, substrate) vary with size of body of water, and whether pike are present or absent. One to three smaller males often take part in the spawning act with a single, larger female. A female may spawn with different males. Number of eggs per female varies from approximately 36,000 to 200,000. New is the idea that females develop two clutches of eggs which are spawned approximately two weeks apart. No nest is built, the eggs are scattered over the bottom, and no parental care or protection is provided eggs or young. Spawning time is the only period when numbers of individuals are in close proximity to one another. It is felt that body contact at this time is the

Exhibiting the voracity that will eventually make him a feared predator, a young musky holds a minnow sideways before swallowing it. With appropriate food, a young musky can measure 10 to 12 inches long by November of its first year.

mechanism by which the unsightly, cancerous disease, Lymphocarcoma, is transferred from one individual to another. Muskellunge are particularly susceptible to this problem, but an infection is not always fatal. When spawning takes place on flooded shorelines there is a risk that the eggs or young could be stranded by lowering water levels. The highly organic nature of the substrate of certain spawning grounds also poses a threat to survival of eggs and newly hatched young. Survival from egg to adult is extremely low.

Hatching takes place in eight to 14 days depending on water temperature. The young remain inactive on the substrate for a further 10 days deriving nutrients from the yolksac. After that period they become free swimming and feed on crustacean, planktonic organisms. Within two weeks they are feeding on the young of other fishes and survival probably depends on the hatching time of the forage species coinciding with the switch from plankton to fish. As the muskellunge grows the diet becomes predominantly fish, with less frequent food items being any other vertebrate animal so incautious as to be in or on the water. The preferred food for adult muskellunge is moderately large soft-rayed fishes. Such a meal can take as much as two days to digest, during which time the muskellunge is probably sedentary in some kind of protective cover.

Muskellunge are not adapted to protracted swimming or excessive struggle. As a consequence, they are vulnerable to angling fatigue, particularly when high water temperatures make it difficult to overcome oxygen debt resulting from excessive activity. Muskellunge are sight and sprint predators. Body shape, eye location, and position of unpaired fins are highly adapted to this mode of feeding.

If adequate and appropriate food is available, growth rate is rapid and by November of the first year the young muskellunge are 10 to 12 inches long. Growth remains relatively rapid until the attainment of sexual maturity and then rate decreases. As the fish gets older the rate of increase in length decreases steadily and the increase in weight becomes more significant, especially in females. Maximum size and weight and longevity are greater for females than for males and almost all record fish are females.

In the past, when ages were derived from scales, it was assumed that 18 to 20 years of age was the maximum. Aging individuals from cleithral bones has made it obvious that some fish live to be at least 30 years of age. In the past, minimum size limits allowed muskellunge to be killed at ages of four to seven years, thereby preventing contribution to the population over a possible additional period of 20 to 23 years. More recent decisions to increase minimum size limits, and the adoption of catch and release angling should have a very beneficial effect on populations. This is particularly true since most muskellunge kept were kept as trophies and trophy fishing is highly selective of large females, the best contributors to recruitment. Catch and release is, however, a two-edged sword in that it makes far fewer specimens available for study, and the development of management strategies for particular waters. We still know very little about the reproductive capacity of the largest and oldest individuals, and whether true senescence occurs.

PIONEER MUSKY MANAGEMENT

Fish populations by themselves are fairly easy to manage if two major factors are favorable — habitat and human population. Practically all problems in managing lakes and streams for better fishing are man-made. The investigation of most "poor fishing" complaints most often discloses that the original problem is the result of actions of people who have misunderstood and mistreated the resource. Fish professionals are more proficient in working out solutions to a current problem, be it musky, walleye, or bass, than they are in handling the cause — human beings.

In the early days of artificial fish propagation and stocking, a decade or so before the turn of the century and for some years after, the products coming from the first fish hatcheries and deposited in hundreds of waters across the country were really not indispensable. Effective regulations, and their enforcement, for the protection and harvesting of fish by commercial fishermen and anglers would have been sufficient without a large scale stocking program, considering the pollution-free waters of that era and the demographics of the human population. Now, nearly 100 years later, the reverse is true. Almost all waters have been badly treated, actually abused, to the extent that the natural reproduction of fish, with few exceptions, has been reduced to less than half of their normal potential.

The initial mission perceived by those early fisheries professionals — stocking — is of higher priority today than it was in 1900. Present day anglers would have slim pickings for muskies were it not for those early decisions and for present fish stocking programs.

Oddly, what it took nearly a century to bring about was not intended to be that way. Greater musky stocking efforts have come about as a result of physical and biological degradation of lakes and streams was the exploitation of the existing fish resource, especially musky populations, first by commercial fishing and spearing and, later, by thousands of anglers who became more mobile and better equipped than ever before. Were it not for the breadth of knowledge gained from years of research and pioneer manage-

Stocking hatchery-raised muskies is more important now than ever before because of biological degradation of lakes and streams and increasing demand on the resource.

ment, as well as today's continuing intensive management, the lakes and streams in Musky Country would probably be unable to cope with the demand.

Originally, the natural reproduction of muskellunge in its North American range, although classically accepted as poor, was generally adequate to provide balanced supplies of muskies and their prey species in most waters. However, for varying reasons, habitat deterioration compounded by excessive harvest (mostly commercial) imposed extreme conditions that led to overexploitation and depletion of muskellunge. At that point, stocking was mandated and triggered what can be historically perceived as the first muskellunge management approach.

Although fish culture is only a means to an end, not an end in itself, probably one of the most enduring contributions to the future conservation of muskellunge is the hatchery. In the final analysis, when the last spawning area has been spoiled by outboard motors, chemicals and landfills, the preservation of muskellunge will depend on the continuing application of accumulated knowledge and production expertise in hatcheries. Wisconsin's Fish Management Division pointed out in 1965 that "Historically, stocking has progressed from overoptimism through disillusionment to the present stage in which it is one of several important tools of the fish manager. Used with hard-nosed realism, stocking can produce relatively efficient results."

By definition, modern fish management encompasses all administrative actions and procedures designed and implemented, generally by a government agency, to restore, maintain and/or enhance the biological and economic potential of fish species in any given body of water. The terminology changes to fisheries management when multiple species are collectively considered in expansive water areas, such as the Great Lakes fisheries, the Atlantic Coast fisheries or the inland waters fisheries of Wisconsin. When considered together, the sport fishery and the commercial fishery, for example become segments of the Great Lakes fisheries. So, muskellunge management can be considered a single species endeavor and a significant part of the larger picture of a fisheries management program that is regulated by sound biological, political and economic principles and objectives.

Guided by my definition of fish management, six major approaches to muskellunge management can be identified in North American waters as they occurred in the past century:

1. Propagation and stocking
2. Regulation (harvest restrictions)
3. Classification of waters
4. Research
5. Population control and reclamation
6. Habitat preservation and protection

Probably the first record of one of the tools of muskellunge management, as we now define it, was reported by W. O. Ayres in the *Proceedings of the The Boston Society of Natural History (1851-1854)* where muskellunge, then classified as *Esox Nobilior*, were introduced into a pond near Bellows Falls, Massachusetts. When an embankment broke loose, the fish escaped into the Connecticut River. Whether this accidental release was successful is not known.

As human settlement and development progressed in the 19th century, the states and provinces adjacent to the Great Lakes and the St. Lawrence River were naturally among the first to recognize the depletion of fish stocks. They, along with the federal governments of the United States and Canada, were the first logical forerunners of fisheries management by enacting legislation to control the commercial harvest of muskellunge for market and to establish regulations for anglers seeking this species. Thus, protective legislation governing the harvest of fish, along with stocking, was one of the primary tools of early muskellunge management.

In his description of muskellunge management in Ohio, Clarence F. Clark tells of an abundance of Great Lakes muskellunge *(Esox masquinongy masquinongy)* in Sandusky Bay in 1830 and that spawning runs up the Cuyahoga, the Maumee, Sandusky and Vermilion rivers indicated a large, widely distributed population. Clark stated in 1964 that "although the large population in Lake Erie appears to have been drastically reduced during the first half of the 19th century, a remnant population of unknown size has remained." In 1941, a commercial fisherman said that between 1902 and 1905 as many as 100 muskellunge were caught in Maumee Bay (Toledo) in a single day but since then the species has decreased and appears to be absent. Milton B. Trautman, author of *The Fishes of Ohio*, considered the population of muskellunge in Lake Erie to be so reduced in numbers by 1950 "as to be in danger or extirpation." The Ohio Fish Commission report of 1875-1876 stated that small muskellunge (1 1/2 to two pounds) sold in a Cleveland fish market for 8 cents per pound but "larger fish of about 15 pounds brought five dollars." The largest specimen from Ohio waters of Lake Erie was described in 1891 by Lewis M. McCormick as being six feet long and weighing 78 pounds.

Another indication of 19th century muskellunge abundance was the early commercial fishing for this species as reported in *Fresh Water Fishes of Canada* by Scott and Crossman. Between 1870 and 1900 thousands of pounds of muskellunge were marketed annually in Quebec and Ontario because of their size and quality of their flesh. In 1868 one Ontario catch recorded from Lake Simcoe totaled 229,050 pounds. Also in Ontario, the annual catch in 1890 was 651,406 pounds, mostly from one lake (Scugog). Commercial fishing for muskellunge was discontinued in Ontario in 1904 mainly due to an increase in angling interest. Commercial fishing continued in Quebec until at least 1936.

In the book *Man Against Musky*, Howard M. Levy tells about an afternoon catch in November 1932 of more than 900 pounds by a market fisherman on Chautauqua Lake in New York. Thirty fish averaged 30 pounds each. Levy said "during the Depression Years and prior to that time, fishing for the market was allowed on Chautauqua Lake, with virtually no restrictions as to size, limit or season (rod and reel was, however, required). The market fisherman, while possibly realizing some enjoyment in his work was, nevertheless, primarily interested in the financial returns from his catch. Late fall and winter live bait fishing (in the 1930s) both from boats and through the ice, produced fabulous catches, most of the fish being heavy females, the backbone of the brood stock. It is no wonder, then, that the 'lunge population of Chautauqua Lake by the mid-1930s dwindled to the point of extinction ..."

Other states having native muskellunge waters were undoubtedly heavily exploited; however, the extent of the commercial harvest in Michigan, Wisconsin and Minnesota was poorly documented but the few records we have shed some light on uncontrolled muskellunge harvest which may or may not have been commercial.

Extremely heavy angling harvest of muskellunge was extant in the 1880s and 1890s in Michigan, Wisconsin and Minnesota by only a limited number of fishermen. By virtue of their abundance in those years, muskellunge were easily taken by anglers using "primitive" fishing gear — spoon hooks, heavy cord lines, home-fashioned steel leaders and cane poles. Many small groups of anglers caught 50 to 100 muskies weighing several hundred pounds in only two to three days. Keep in mind that in most states and provinces at that time, laws on muskellunge harvest were practically non-existent. And where there were laws, there was no effort at enforcement.

Though the little girl at left was shy about having her photo taken, these four couples were proud to display their catch of muskies and northern pike. Scenes like this were common at the beginning of the 20th century.

In the August 1901 edition of *Outing*, a sportsman's magazine of that era, Emerson Hough reported in his article "Angling in the Midwest," that muskellunge fishing in the Midwestern states was on the decline. He provides such an interesting documentation of early day musky fishing that I feel obligated to include it in this historical setting.

"In regard to the angling for muscallunge, one is obligated to write somewhat in the past tense. We still have muscallunge fishing in Wisconsin, though little or none in Michigan. Minnesota has a number of muscallunge waters within her borders and indeed is today attracting the greater portion of the attention of the trolling cult. Yet, prolific as are these waters, there is no comparing the results of today with those which were common ten, fifteen or twenty years ago. Pen cannot chronicle the unspeakable butchery which took place over all the Wisconsin wilderness when the railroads first penetrated that virgin country. Never has the brutishness of human nature been more fully exemplified than it was up in the dark forest of the pine country, which was at that time but little known. It was exceeding simple. One went up the railroad to almost any little logging town, took a little-used trail to almost any little lake tributary to the Mississippi River system, anywhere in the Manitowish, Turtle Lake, Tomahawk Lake, or St. Germain region, indeed on any one of those lakes which drain into the Wisconsin or the Flambeau River, and having secured any kind of a boat from a birch bark to a lumbering bateau, he simply took to trolling almost any kind of a spoon hook in almost any part of the lake. The merest novice might take a dozen, a score, indeed two scores of magnificent muscallunge in a day's fishing, if he did not tire out. One party composed of men from Louisville, Ky., and from Chicago, on one trip piled up over a ton of muscallunge on the sandy shores of one of the lakes near Three Rivers, Wis. They returned year after year and repeated their shameless performances, until at length even the guides revolted and told them that they must come there no more. A great deal of this was hand line fishing, without the first element of sport attached to it. One learned gentleman, who adorns the medical fraternity in the city of Chicago, invented a sort of spring box, so arranged in the stern of the boat that when a muscallunge struck the spoon he found himself played automatically on a big coiled spring, like a mammoth watch spring. By means of this contrivance, with the hand line in one hand and a couple of poles sticking out over the side of the boat, this gentleman angler managed to satisfy his idea of sport. No one can tell how many tons of fish this one party of ruffians have killed ...

"Today we do not hear of thirty or forty pound muscallunge as a

The number of muskies in Musky Country seemed endless to the sportsmen at the beginning of the 20th century. Here, Silas Sayner with the results of "a typical day of fishing," as the writing on the back of the photo says.

common thing in Wisconsin. The fish run very much smaller and very much fewer ... Really I doubt if there was a fish taken over forty pounds in Wisconsin last season, and perhaps not a half a dozen, recorded or unrecorded, that went over thirty pounds. The largest muscallunge of which I have ever heard in these waters weighed fifty-five pounds and it was taken some fifteen years ago.

"In Minnesota the muscallunge traffic set in at a much later date than it did in Wisconsin, hence the angler found a region in which the lumbering operations had been well advanced for many years and where lumbermen and Indians had done their endeavor to keep the muscallunge supply from becoming too great ... "

After a little reflection on the statement that "One party ... on one trip piled up over a ton of muscallunge ...," it takes little imagination to conclude that these numbers had to be for commercial purposes.

In his paper *The Propagation of Muskellunge in Wisconsin*, published in the American Fisheries Society Transactions of 1901, Superintendent James Nevin confirmed conditions that were then leading to rampant muskellunge harvest: "For many years since the wilderness of northern Wisconsin was opened by the railways and by lumbering operations; with the advent of the comforts and conveniences which the railroad takes into a new country, and the encroachment of the settler and summer hotel on the primitive banks of our northern lakes, the pursuit of the muskellunge has been constant and relentless. Its utter extermination has been well nigh accomplished in many of our lakes to which it is indigenous and nearly all of our waters have been cleared of this fish to such an extent that its future has become a matter of much concern to sportsmen, fish culturists and others interested in keeping our waters well-stocked with superior game fish."

So, the consequences of unsparing commercial fishing and exorbitant angling pressures were primary factors in prompting the earliest efforts at muskellunge management.

What is the nature of this beast? Why all the continental interest in this bronzed member of the pike family? It's an easy answer: We are talking about the largest fresh water game fish in the United States — next to the sturgeons!

National attention afforded the claimed 69-pound, 15-ounce world record muskellunge in 1957 (which stood until being proven a hoax in 1992), and the actual world record 69-pound, 11-ounce muskellunge, prompted previously dormant states to active management programs for this species. This was motivated by demands form their sportsmen to manage a trophy species which had all but disappeared in inland waters of the states of Kentucky, Michigan, Minnesota, Ohio, Pennsylvania and Tennessee.

Blessed with more expansive and remote water areas, greater musky stocks and less pressure, the Canadian provinces have been in less jeopardy. The Kawartha Lakes area in southeastern Ontario was an exception. The present situation shows that those agencies which have lagged in trophy musky production and/or management, have now been prodded into action. But, competition for anglers' dollars has also prompted many non-musky states to move into the trophy fish arena.

Musky hunters can take solace in the present status of native muskellunge populations in at least eight states (Kentucky, Michigan, Minnesota, New York, Ohio, Pennsylvania, Tennessee and Wisconsin). Even in view of increased angling pressure, this fish appears to be thriving. This may seem a paradoxical situation considering the high angling exploitation and loss of musky habitat from excessive human development. These states, with more sophisticated methods of propagation, stocking and other improved management tools, have not only been able to maintain trophy fishing, but have extended the musky's range to provide greater opportunities for this type of angling. At this time, musky stocking, as an effective and heavily used procedure, appears to be the most significant management contribution to healthy musky populations.

The best testimonial for the position of muskies in the trophy fish arena is the rapidity with which many "non-musky" states have added this battler to their piscatorial offerings. Consider that nearly a dozen states, where muskies were not indigenous, now have active management programs to attract anglers with this new prize. Four decades ago the states of Colorado, Illinois, Indiana, Iowa, Missouri, Nebraska, New Jersey, North and South Dakota and West Virginia, had no native muskellunge but have since made successful introductions. So much for setting the stage for the management of this fresh water barracuda.

Since the turn of the century until the 1950s, only two states and the province of Ontario made any appreciable effort in the management of muskellunge. The direction of these early programs was confined, in the main, to artificial propagation and stocking efforts. The fish hatchery program of the U. S. Government did not include muskellunge until the early 1950s. Also of primary importance in these first musky conservation programs, was the establishment of seasons, size and bag limits. Wisconsin set its first angling season for muskies in 1889 (closed from February 1 to May 1). New York had similar regulations for Chautauqua Lake at about the same time.

New York began its muskellunge propagation and stocking program at Chautauqua Lake (Bemus Point) in 1887. Wisconsin followed shortly after. In those states artificial musky propagation methods were fairly similar then, consisting of musky egg collection, incubation and hatching. Both states obtained their musky eggs by setting nets in shallow water areas of native musky lakes to capture brood fish after ice-out, from mid-April through early May, dependent upon water temperatures. Rising temperatures above 48 degrees Fahrenheit attracted and concentrated spawners for easy entrapment. In New York, musky spawning operations are still conducted on Chautauqua Lake annually as they were 100 years ago when "pound" nets were set adjacent to known musky spawning shorelines.

Wisconsin's first spawntakers used "fyke" nets in Tomahawk, Minocqua and Kawaguesaga Lakes in 1898.

Both pound nets and fyke nets have the advantage over other types of netting gear by trapping and keeping fish free-swimming and alive. Fyke nets are long bag nets supported by frames and hoops kept in

Wisconsin fish biologists cradle an egg-laden female musky prior to taking spawn for hatchery purposes.

position by a stake and an anchor. They are very portable and can be reset in a matter of minutes. Pound nets are fish traps consisting of a netting arranged into a directing wing and an enclosure with a narrow entrance and are held stationary between four or five stakes. Although they are far less portable, pound nets will entrap and hold greater numbers of muskies than a fyke net. In contrast with New

York's one-lake operation, Wisconsin conducts egg procurement annually from 10 to 12 out of about 600 musky lakes available in the northern third of the state.

Beside the artificial propagation of muskellunge in New York and Wisconsin before 1900 (Pennsylvania attempted it at their Corry Hatchery in the 1890s but discontinued), Ontario followed suit in 1927; Pennsylvania and Ohio in 1953; West Virginia and North Dakota in 1958.

Wisconsin's early leadership in musky culture was undisputed. Its first techniques were only slightly changed from the 1958 practices described by Leon Johnson:

"The first muskellunge are taken in the nets when waters reach 42 degrees. The greatest numbers of muskellunge with easily-taken ripe eggs which have the highest percentage hatch are taken when the waters range from 48 to 56 F.

"The large proportion of male muskellunge found in lakes is an advantageous situation because as many as six males may be needed to produce sufficient milt for the eggs from a single female. Lakes that contain predominantly large-sized female muskellunge enable the spawn-takers to obtain the required eggs from relatively few fish, since one large female will often produce up to four quarts of eggs.

"Muskellunge that produce large eggs are preferred to those that produce small eggs. Large eggs with a greater store of food materials in the yolksac produce larger, stronger fry that have a better chance for survival. Size of water-hardened muskellunge eggs may range from 0.130 inch to 0.100 inch diameter, which is 30,801 to 67,670 eggs per liquid quart, respectively.

A large female musky is stripped of spawn by fish biologists.

"Female muskellunge are checked at the netting site to determine if eggs will flow freely from the vent. Ripe females are retained in a large tank carried in the boat and occasionally are replaced in the nets until the next day if sufficient males are not available.

"The sufficient spawning of muskellunge is accomplished by the spawn-taker with the assistance of a helper. The females and males are placed together in a large tank in the boat and taken to shore for the actual spawn-taking. A small porcelain pan is rinsed in the lake water and placed on a small stand that holds the pan in position without spilling eggs, even though the muskellunge may thrash. The spawner and helper lift the female from the tank and hold the muskellunge in position over the dry pan for the stripping process. If a muskellunge has more available eggs than the pan can hold, the female is placed back in the tank until there is time to take more eggs.

"Male muskellunge produce only small quantities of milt, less than 0.3 cc., which is usually measured by the number of drops. Several males are used to minimize the failure to impregnate eggs due to the use of an impotent male. The ratio of sexes has been 61 percent males to 39 percent females, in Wisconsin lakes. The eggs and milt are stirred with the fingers to assure adequate mixing and are washed immediately with lake water. The lake water activates the sperm and fertilization occurs. An experienced spawning crew performs the stripping and fertilization of muskellunge eggs in about three minutes. Washed eggs are immediately poured on floating screen trays in a tub of lake water to expand and water-harden without disturbance for at least 15 minutes. Twenty minutes to six hours later the egg screens are bundled together in an angle iron case, submerged in a tank of fresh lake water on a truck, and transported to the hatchery.

"Upon arrival at the hatchery the muskellunge eggs are measured volumetrically and introduced into four-quart hatching jars for incubation. Each jar is usually reserved for the eggs of an individual muskellunge provided there are enough eggs to ensure their rolling freely in the moving waters. The usual quantity is from 1 1/2 quarts to 2 quarts of eggs per hatchery jar, the egg size averaging about 50,000 per quart. Water temperatures that normally range through 50 degrees to 70 degrees Fahrenheit bring on an 85 to 95 percent hatch of muskellunge sac fry from the eggs within 12 to 13 days. Incubation at the higher tem-peratures appears to result in normal fry. Muskellunge eggs hatch more slowly at low water temperatures and are subject to higher mortalities.

"Newly hatched muskellunge sac-fry are held in the jars for an additional 10 to 14 days until the yolk sac is almost gone, and the fry have increased to the approximate 0.5-inch length of the "swim-up" stage. Retaining screens at the top of the hatching jars are removed and the muskellunge fry are allowed to swim up and out of the jar overflow. The fry are caught and held in screen boxes in fresh circulating water. Swim-up fry are removed from the screen boxes when sufficient numbers have collected."

An old practice followed by Wisconsin, New York, and Ontario fish culturists was to float the eggs on screen trays for incubation in troughs until the hatch was completed. Dead eggs and those containing fungus were removed with a "picker." The dormant sac fry were stocked shortly after hatching, a questionable procedure at this vulnerable stage and one that modern fish managers would frown upon. Hatching jars were also used for incubating musky eggs during this period but the nearly immobile sac fry were removed for stocking immediately after hatching and long before the swim-up stage.

In Wisconsin, from 1875 to 1939, muskies were stocked by popular demand and pressures from various sources, most of which lacked any kind of biological justi-fication. Even with very low survival such distribution procedures undoubtedly led to the first man-made extension of the musky's native range.

From 1900 to 1912, Wisconsin's first permanent warm-water hatchery built at Woodruff produced and stocked 103,745,000 muskellunge. These fish were shipped as two- or three-day-old fry and were stocked following delivery to cooperators and applicants who received allotments from a fish car at railroad stations. Other applicants hauled their allotments directly from the hatchery to local lakes with their own buggies and wagons. The newly hatched fry were placed in 10-gallon milk cans with numbers ranging from 3,000 to 5,000 per can. In addition to lakes and streams along rail lines, many waters within close wagon-hauling distance of the hatcheries were stocked in this manner. Other agencies propagating muskies at that time followed similar methods of distribution until aerated tank trucks were put into service in the early 1930s.

Hatchery-raised musky fingerlings are inspected by a worker.

It was too much to expect that stocking, a single tool of fish management, could remedy the complex problems of all lakes and streams. Resorts and business interests felt otherwise, however. Better fishing bolstered the economy, they figured, so any effort to suppress fish stocking was severely challenged and, in Wisconsin, the Conservation Department was pressured to increase fish planting.

After reaching the department's fish production goal of one billion (predominantly fry sizes) in 1937, the Fisheries Propagation Division repeated the record annually until 1940 when a new record of 1.5 billion fish was produced and distributed. But this was the turning point!

Under Dr. E. A. Birge, University of Wisconsin researchers had uncovered many of the limnological aspects of northern Wisconsin lakes but they had not focused on the relationship of these scientific factors to the fish populations in those waters.

Recognizing the need to translate some of this academic data to practical fish management, Conservation Director H. W. McKenzie ordered the creation of a new fishery unit to provide answers to prevailing lake and stream problems. The new unit was named the Fishery Biology Division. In 1937 aquatic biologists were placed in three locations in the state where lake and stream surveys were initiated and recommendations based on research data began to have a greater impact on stocking procedures. The new division provided a means of evaluating on-going practices in fish management and played an important role in changing the direction of future stocking practices.

By 1939, an awareness of the waste in indiscriminate fish stocking brought to light the weakness of some techniques, particularly the stocking of two- to three-day-old fry which are extremely vulnerable to predation and severe environmental fluctuations.

The first step in controlling this massive fish-stocking panacea was to establish a fish quota system in 1938. Chemical, physical and biological factors affecting lakes, fish species present and angling pressure were taken into consideration before fish allotments were determined. Planting receipts requiring cooperator's signatures were introduced to keep better records for each body of water stocked. This was the turning point in the use of this management tool which led to Wisconsin's first warm-water fish stocking policy.

The new statewide policy, which greatly curtailed fry plantings of warm water gamefish, created new objectives for Wisconsin musky hatcheries at Woodruff and Spooner. Lake and stream surveys revealed the need to make an adjustment in existing programs, mainly to stock larger-sized warm water gamefish. The net result was to reduce the total number of fish stocked but to improve the quality of fish produced — from fry to fingerling.

The pond rearing of muskellunge to large-sized fingerlings was initiated in 1926 at Woodruff when 1,600 fingerlings, six to 10 inches in size, were raised. Numbers of muskellunge fingerlings produced in rearing ponds were limited and erratic until more systematic procedures in handling fry and managing rearing ponds were developed. Only 7,020 musky fingerlings were pond reared and stocked from 1926 to 1939. Musky sac fry were stocked in the ponds in the spring along with forage fish and ponds were merely "observed" until early fall harvest. This "planting and harvest" cycle was changed to a precise sequence of providing plankton food initially, then forage of fry size, larger fry forage and finally minnows plus an orderly schedule of pond preparation, daily management and seasonal evaluation.

Wisconsin was the first state to report a successful extensive musky pond rearing program that covered a six-year period from 1942 to 1947. Even with the restrictions imposed by the onset of World War II, the Woodruff

Hatchery responded by producing a record 33,639 musky fingerlings in its rearing program in 1942. Many new techniques were developed in the ensuing years. Strong, healthy fry were retained in hatching jars, aquaria and screen boxes until reaching the swim-up stage prior to release in prime condition to rearing ponds. Subsequently, a rearing pond management regimen evolved that included eradication of predacious insects, chemical control of undesirable aquatic plants and algae, and improved pond stocking rates for muskies and forage fish. Drainable rearing ponds at Woodruff and Spooner range in size from .08 acre to six acres with water depths of 18 inches to four feet from inlet to outlet.

During the early success with muskellunge pond rearing, the emphasis was on numbers as well as size of fish. The efficiency of rearing pond production was determined largely by the percentage of fingerlings produced from the initial fry stocking. Muskellunge fry stocked in ponds produced fingerlings at an average survival rate of about 35 percent. Large numbers of fingerling muskies were reared at the two major hatcheries located at Woodruff and Spooner. The magnitude of the muskellunge rearing program is reflected in annual production which ranged from 30,216 to 477,528 fingerlings in a 10-year period, from 1950 to 1959.

In 1954, pond-rearing goals were shifted to total weight produced rather than numbers of muskellunge fingerlings reared. Small muskellunge fingerlings (three to six inches long) were then regarded as a by-product of the rearing operation and were cropped as the rearing season progressed. In this manner a more adequate food supply was assured the fish remaining in the ponds so that larger, heavier specimens were reared. This increased weight program progressed from 2,590 pounds in 1957 to 14,700 pounds of eight- to 12-inch fingerlings coming out of the Woodruff ponds in 1969. More than 2 million musky fingerlings were reared and planted between 1941 and 1969.

The new production goal forced full realization of supplying the demand for forage minnows to feed young muskellunge for it is still the primary key to successful fingerling production. An analysis of muskellunge pond production records at the Woodruff station showed that four to five pounds of minnows are required to produce one pound of muskellunge. To achieve conversion ratios in this range requires a surplus of available forage minnows of required sizes throughout a 4 1/2-month rearing season.

The efficiency of muskellunge rearing pond production in Wisconsin is reflected in the results of 10 acres of rearing pond area at Woodruff which have produced an average of 7,500 muskellunge fingerlings per acre. Weight of muskellunge fingerlings produced in Wisconsin rearing ponds has ranged from 200 pounds to 800 pounds per acre per year. Remember that the rearing ponds do not produce all the food required for muskellunge and that most of the food consumed by these fish are placed in them daily throughout the season.

The two major muskellunge hatcheries in Wisconsin are supplied with water from natural lakes and a stream impoundment. Water from these sources has presented problems in erratic temperatures and quality for incubation of muskellunge eggs. High mortalities resulted from weak fry and differential hatching resulted from excessively high and low water temperatures. To prevent future muskellunge mortalities, Wisconsin constructed a hatchery at Woodruff with equipment designed to overcome some of these problems. Installation of similar equipment was made for the Spooner Hatchery after final testing at Woodruff.

Initial studies in 1957 with a closed circuit hatching jar battery for the incubation and hatching of muskellunge eggs showed that it was feasible to achieve temperature control in a jar-type hatchery system. In 1962, a 12-jar experimental battery, equipped with an electrically-controlled valve, mixed hot water of a constant temperature so that cold lake water of a varying temperature in the proper amounts could provide a desired minimum temperature. After three years of experimental incubating and hatching of northern pike and muskellunge eggs, hatching batteries were designed using the temperature control equipment which had proved successful. This new equipment was incorporated in a new 1,100-jar warm water game fish hatchery which was constructed and completed in 1961-1964 at Woodruff. The new hatchery was supplied with a maximum of 2,350 gallons of water per minute. The main feature was a temperature controlled muskellunge hatching battery consisting of 60 jars which collectively received 120 g.p.m. of water. Both hot and cold water were forced to this battery by a centrifugal pump and automatic temperature control equipment regulated the desired temperatures for effective incubating and hatching.

By fine regulation of water temperature, closer coordination of the hatching and rearing functions in muskellunge propagation was achieved. Providing consistent hatches of strong, healthy muskellunge fry regardless of weather conditions followed. Since excessive and catastrophic mortalities of the past were avoided in succeeding years, this development was regarded as an outstanding achievement.

Muskellunge hatches can now be regulated to coordinate with other events in the rearing process. The hatchery man can plan ahead and prepare rearing ponds because fry hatching dates can be calculated and the exact time required for yolksac assimilation determined to facilitate stocking in rearing ponds. Fry stocking can thus be accomplished when the plankton pulse is on the increase and be timed to relate to the hatching of suckers and other forage fish so essential to their early welfare. The temperature control measures permit operation of a better pond feeding regimen also. After a short cycle of feeding on zooplankton, young muskellunge consume large numbers of sucker fry. Since larval suckers grow rapidly in rearing ponds after hatching it is necessary to time the stocking of swim-up muskellunge fry so that the sucker fry can be readily captured and eaten by them. The control temperature battery also allows timing of the sucker hatch to coincide with feeding requirements.

Bringing off an earlier hatch in cold spring weather by regulating water temperature during incubation also provides for a longer rearing period. From one to two weeks of additional growth can be gained by early hatching of muskellunge. It is estimated that the extra one to two weeks of growth on 30,000 muskellunge fingerlings reared until mid-October would produce approximately an extra ton of muskellunge flesh and from one to 1 1/2 inches of length per fingerling. Since size is a critical factor in the success of muskellunge stocking, the extra rearing time is particularly advantageous.

Controlled water temperatures at the Woodruff Hatchery have assured a steady production of strong

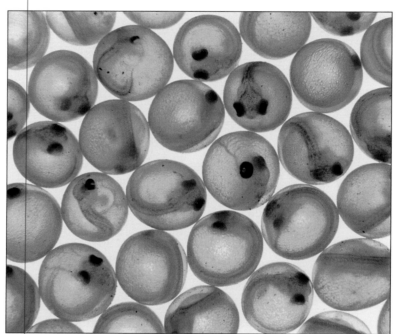

By controlling the water temperature in the hatcheries, biologists discovered they could hatch muskellunge eggs successfully regardless of the outside weather.

muskellunge swim-up fry. Methods of controlling temperatures by heating and mixing water for fry production have proven highly effective and optimum temperature ranges for incubating and hatching muskellunge eggs appear to be in a gradient starting from 52 degrees Fahrenheit and peaking at about 60 degrees.

Massive muskellunge fry mortalities at the Woodruff Hatchery occurred several times during the 20-year interval from 1943 to1963. It was suspected that these mortalities were caused by an abnormal water temperatures and possibly water quality. The presence of copper and zinc in the hatchery water supply was reported by Gilbert Radonski in 1964 and 1965. Copper appeared to be toxic at the relatively low concentration of 100 parts per billion. Since copper and zinc go into solution with a low pH and are more toxic in soft water than hard water, Radonski suggested a change in pH could alter the toxicity of these metals. The temperature control system warm water outlet provided water with a higher pH than natural cold water, thus neutralizing the effect of the toxins. The maintenance of minimum water temperatures (above 50 degrees) by automatic temperature control thus provided an additional safeguard in muskellunge egg incubation. The disappearance of muskellunge fry mortalities at the Woodruff Hatchery since the installation of temperature control testifies to the elimination of this cause of mortality. Hatchery innovations were responsible.

The Woodruff staff learned in 1956 that Quebec, New York, Pennsylvania and Ohio had been experimenting with troughs and tanks for rearing muskies instead of ponds, feeling that reducing the size of the rearing area permitted better observation and more exact control. To test this new technique, 14-foot rearing tanks holding about 12 inches of water were used as troughs. Swim-up musky fry were fed live food such as daphnia, sucker fry and minnows with attendant daily feeding, sorting and tank cleaning. The results of this intensive tank culture experiment over a two-year period offered considerable promise as a muskellunge rearing procedure. The new technique was particularly effective in increasing survival rates of muskies in the fry and early fingerling stages when most mortality occurs in rearing ponds. Losses in ponds averaged about 70 percent compared to the

44 percent average loss experienced in the tank experiment. However, while survival rates from fry to fingerlings were greatly improved, growth rates for young muskies held in tanks for two to three months were considerably lower than their pond-reared counterparts. The small muskies grew three to five inches in tanks, far from reaching the six to eight inches the pond-reared fish that the fish manager's stocking plans called for. But, muskies held in tanks and fed zooplankton for two to three weeks after the swim-up stage provided a means to carry the fry through their most vulnerable phase. All Wisconsin stations now obtain large numbers of vigorous 1 1/2-inch to three-inch fingerlings for transfer to ponds for extended rearing using this system.

So, even though other states developed successful, sophisticated systems for tank-trough-rearing hybrids and purebred muskies, they were unable to match Wisconsin's total annual production of over 100,000 purebred musky fingerlings.

The year 1962 was a record breaker at the Woodruff hatchery. A news release announced the year's accomplishments:

"Madison, Wis. — Another world record in muskellunge production came out of a Wisconsin Conservation Department hatchery this season for the second year in a row.

In 1961 the Spooner hatchery turned out 4,216 pounds, more than had ever been reared at a single installation. This year the Woodruff hatchery astonished propagation experts throughout the country by more than doubling that figure with an unprecedented 10,714 pounds. In both cases the records were established with no increase in personnel and little or no expansion of facilities. Total production for the state this year is more than 12,000 pounds. The last of these muskies — some 280,000 — were stocked in Wisconsin waters this month.

"The fish themselves are the kind that please not only the hatchery man, but the angler and biologist as well. The bulk range from four to 14 inches in length — survival size that research has shown grow to span 30 inches and take a belt at a bucktail.

"At Woodruff, Northeast Area Fisheries Supervisor Art Oehmcke said 75 percent of the credit for the big success goes to hatchery foreman Kenneth Walker.

"'Walker's timing, observation and management, coupled with a few gimmicks gleaned from experience and research gave us our best year and we're hoping we've found the formula that will keep production at this level,' Oehmcke said."

Some exemplary achievements in fish production records were evident in the 20 years following the completion of the new hatchery. Mingled with these successes were procedural problems which today shed an ominous light on an insidious environmental degradation of the drainage area above the Woodruff hatchery.

A review of hatchery figures for walleye and muskellunge fingerlings reared for those two decades reveals a much greater yield than was experienced for the years between the 1930s and the 1960s.

The fish production charts for the period 1970 through 1988 disclose an output of 2,126,674 muskellunge fingerlings weighing 234,454 pounds, a huge increase from the previous 18-year period.

While the overall rearing pond effort was noteworthy, the incubation and hatching process at the Woodruff hatchery became erratic due to subtle, pernicious ecological shifts in the lake and watershed above it.

Accelerated erosion and nutrients resulting from shoreline property "improvement" and highly intensive recreational use of the three headwater lakes led to an increase in sedimentation and a reduction in the water quality and volume from Madeline Lake. The major impact of this deterioration was a harmful increase in water temperature in the Woodruff hatchery during the month of May when walleye and sucker hatching is at its peak. Normal incubation and hatching temperatures should not exceed 62 degrees Fahrenheit.

Ironically, the previously installed control equipment, intended to thwart intolerably low water temperature drops during incubation and hatching in April, was useless for such late spring occurrences.

Fortunately, in September 1989, the Wisconsin DNR initiated a project to evaluate sites for a new hatchery in northern Wisconsin, and explore the possibility of expanding existing facilities to provide the capability of raising additional fingerling walleyes and muskies annually.

In July 1991, the Cooper Engineering Company of Rice Lake, Wisconsin, was awarded the design contract for the DNR's Northern Fish Hatcheries Renovation Project. The main goals for the project were to increase production of extended growth walleye and muskellunge fingerlings in northern Wisconsin lakes, and to ultimately increase sportfishing success in the area. It was the first major attempt by the DNR to increase production of these species since 1965.

Plans for the Woodruff Fish Hatchery were completed in January 1993 and construction started in May. The $3,300,000 renovation includes reshaping the existing muskellunge rearing ponds and providing aeration and internal harvest kettles for those ponds.

The rearing pond water supply is filtered to keep out insects, predatory fish, and unwanted fish eggs. The egg incubation water for the hatchery is fine-filtered to remove remaining organics. A new cold water supply from Clear Lake and state-of-the-art controls and monitoring equipment were added to improve control of the incubation process.

Thus, the conservation administrators and legislators have provided the authority and the means to protect a fish propagation facility which has evolved as a living demonstration of the effects of environmental degradation. Created in 1902 to conserve fish species, the Woodruff Hatchery will continue to make fish cultural contributions into the 21st century!

"The proof in the pudding is in the eating." This quote from Cervantes' Don Quixote is apropos to the muskellunge fishery in Wisconsin in the 1990s. For the practical fish manager, one of the best indicators of fishing success is the satisfied angler. Fishing license sales and annual harvest estimates in Wisconsin attest to this. The present status of muskellunge populations in Wisconsin, even in view of increased angling pressure, appears to be at an all-time high. This situation may seem paradoxical considering the high fishing exploitation and the loss of muskellunge habitat from pollution and excessive human development on lake shores. But, angler success throughout a newly extended range reflects a good fishery. Since muskellunge stocking is the most heavily used management tool, it looms as the most significant management factor!

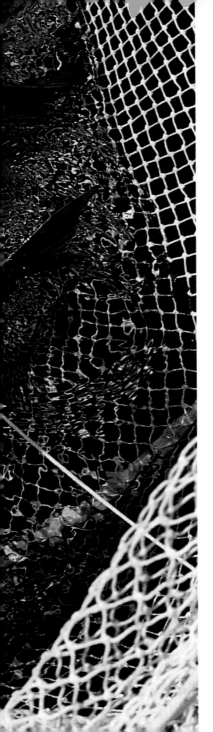

THE ROLE OF RESEARCH

One of the most difficult questions I've had to answer for my children is, "Dad, what do you do for work?" For many occupations this is a relatively easy question. A doctor makes people feel better, a fireman puts out fires, and a carpenter builds things. But how do you explain to a four-year-old what a researcher does, and have him or her understand it?

An explanation of what exactly research is cannot only be difficult in the above situation, but in general is a tough definition to nail down. A fellow researcher defined research this way, "If you know what you're doing, it's not research." Naturally, when I first heard this I laughed. However, after thinking about the phase for a bit, my friend's wisdom became more apparent. The reason we do research is to find answers to questions. In essence, research is exploring the unknown. Hence, muskellunge research may be defined as finding answers to questions using scientific methods to improve the way we manage the muskellunge resource.

How do research studies come about? Most people have seen biologists on a lake in spring or fall sampling fish to collect data for a study. What exactly are they doing? Are these people guided by some logical process which tells them how many fish scales to collect or how many fins to clip?

Actually, the time researchers spend on lakes collecting data is a very small percent of the total time and effort required to conduct a research study. The process of finding solutions to research questions is an experiment or research study. Every research study is designed to address a problem, in this case with muskellunge management. For example, common problems in muskellunge management are low survival of stocked muskellunge or failing natural reproduction.

Once the management problem has been defined, a research study can be constructed to address the problem. For instance, let's use the example of low survival of stocked muskellunge mentioned above and develop a hypothetical research study to investigate the problem.

First, we must gather background information and explore the available data. We may learn from previous studies most of the losses of stocked fish occur between fall (September) and winter (December). We may also find that larger-size fish seem to survive better than smaller ones, and that predator abundance is related to survival. Hence, back-

Preceding pages — Muskies trapped in a fyke net await processing by fisheries biologists.

ground exploration helps researchers avoid "reinventing the wheel."

Let's continue with the study's development. With the knowledge gained with the review of background information, we are able to come up with possible ideas for improving survival. These ideas need to be nurtured and developed. The flow of ideas may go something like this:

Stocked muskellunge are hatched and reared in ponds where no natural fish predators occur. When the time comes for stocking, they are put into a totally new environment where they not only have to search for food but must also avoid becoming food. It may be that the stocked fingerlings are unaware of the dangers that exist in the "real" world and swim their new waters unassumingly as they did in the hatchery pond. Obviously this type of behavior could severely hinder survival chances during the first several days following stocking, and a fingerling may not get a second chance from a hungry predator. Suppose hatchery fingerlings could be conditioned to predators before they are stocked? If some mechanism could be developed where they could be made aware of the inherent dangers to be encountered without being eaten. Maybe the mechanism would be a remote control northern pike (remember, this is a hypothetical study) to chase these young muskellunge around the pond a few days before stocking. In other words, could we "scare the day-lights" out of them and have them live to tell about it?

With background information gathered and ideas generated, the next step is to develop a hypothesis. The hypothesis is an unproven idea which may explain why survival is low. For the above example, the hypothesis could be that conditioning hatchery muskellunge to predators will improve survival.

The study design follows and will test the hypothesis. This is basically how, where and when the study occurs. A properly designed study assures the researcher that when the study is over, he or she can determine if the hypothesis was a correct explanation of the observed phenomenon (low survival is due to unawareness of predators). The design includes such things as the selection of study lakes, sam-

Working as a team, a pair of fisheries biologists records data collected during a study of a musky lake. Later, the data will be analyzed at the biologists' office.

pling techniques, and data collection procedures. When considering experimental design features such as study lakes, selection is based on several criteria. Criteria may include number of lakes needed, types of lakes, size of lakes, species of fish, habitat, and so on. Let's say for this example that the stocking evaluation will include three lakes. Also, because of the available manpower and sampling effort required, lakes need to be less than 500 acres in size. In addition, maybe we are looking at short-term survival in lakes which have no natural reproduction of muskellunge. So a list of candidate lakes are established which meet the selected criteria.

With a study design intact the research study moves into the data collection stage. This phase is the aspect of a study most visible to people because it usually brings researchers onto lakes for their sampling. For the example above, the sampling may consist of determining survival several months after stocking with the use of an electroshocking boat. Electroshocking gear is an effective means to collect young muskellunge without harming them.

Following data collection are the processing and analyzing of the data. This can often be a long and tedious process due to complex statistical procedures. Computer models, bioenergetics, multivariate analysis, discriminate function analysis, and power curves can scare the living daylights out of any normal person, myself included. Nevertheless, proper data analysis is very important because the researcher must accurately interpret the collected data and determine if the study was a success.

The final stage of the research study is termed "technology transfer" or communication. This is when the researchers report their findings to a number of different groups. These groups include other researchers, anglers, and news media. Technology transfer takes the form of written manuscripts for scientific journals, popular articles for outdoor magazines, and interviews with newspaper and television reporters. The main focus here is to get the word out on the research study's results, good or bad. That's right, even a study which has not supported (or proven) the hypothesis needs to be reported. This type of reporting can help guide future research in a direction where chances of finding answers are increased

Muskellunge research is by no means a fad which has developed during the past few years. Actually, early research on muskellunge dates back to the first part of the century. Most early research activities centered around artificial culture and age and growth of muskellunge.

Through time new technologies have developed making more sophisticated studies possible. An example of one advancement in technology which has proved to be an extremely useful tool for muskellunge management is biotelemetry, or telemetry. Telemetry allows researchers to track movements of fish as frequently as they like by receiving a signal from a small battery powered transmitter attached to a fish. Before telemetry, determining many important aspects of muskellunge life history such as movements and behavioral habits were difficult. Muskellunge occur naturally at low densities and are difficult to sample during most of the year. Movements were inferred by marking fish with tags at one time period and recovery of these tags again at a later period. This information answered some questions but left many unanswered. Telemetry has helped define muskellunge spawning habitats, home range, seasonal movements, and behavioral and activity patterns. More recent advancements in telemetry now allow researchers to record information such as heart rate, blood pressure, and

Wearing new "jewelry," a musky just tagged by fish biologists heads for deep water.

water depth and temperature. The use of microprocessors now allows transmitters to be programmed to activate at various times of the year when information is needed. For example, if a study was designed to follow the activity of a fish for a two-week period during the spawning season, the transmitter could be programmed to activate during this time and then shut down for the remainder of the year. This capability could extend the life of transmitters from one year to several years.

The present status of research on the muskellunge involves both traditional studies that better define life history characteristics (e.g. age and growth) along with new technologies that are on the cutting edge of science. An effort to compile all recent and current research on the muskellunge is difficult. Several general categories that provide a brief summary of research and geographic areas (in parentheses) conducting the research follow. Much of this information was generated from an effort by the Esocid Technical Committee (ETC) of the American Fisheries Society. (The Esocid group of fishes includes muskellunge, northern pike and pickerel) In 1992, the ETC sent out a request for information on esocid management and research to all states and provinces which have muskellunge. The information was compiled into a synopsis intended to provide researchers with a current "status report" of what's happening with muskellunge research and management. As mentioned earlier, the initial stages of a research study require the gathering of background information on previous and ongoing research; therefore, it is important for researchers in Iowa to be aware that a study very similar to the one they are about to initiate has recently been completed in New York. This effort is not likely to be all inclusive but should provide a good overview of recent and current research on muskellunge in North America:

• Habitat — Concern for loss and degradation of valuable habitat for muskellunge will be a top research priority for this species in the future. Already many states and provinces are involved in research studies which can identify, protect or rehabilitate critical habitat. Protection of spawning habitat is of paramount importance as muskellunge spawning success has declined dramatically over the recent past. Research studies to identify, quantify, and rehabilitate spawning and nursery areas are in progress in river systems (KY, MN, VA) and lakes (NY, ONT, WI).

• Genetics — Research on genetic aspects of the muskellunge fishery ranks high as a research priority. Philosophies among fisheries personnel have changed recently regarding the protection of "genetic integrity" of our native fisheries, including muskellunge. Genetic integrity could be considered the natural adaptations a population of fish has acquired for survival in a given lake or river system through generations and generations of reproduction. Over time, populations develop a unique arrangement of genetic information which is suited for survival in a specific lake. Muskellunge taken from a different system, for culture purposes, and their offspring stocked into different lakes could prove detrimental to the native population by way of competition and breeding. Evaluation of the performances of different muskellunge strains has been studied for over a decade (MN, WI) but more recent advancements in technologies are allowing fisheries researchers to fine tune this science. Genetic procedures such as protein electrophoresis and DNA analysis are being used to determine the genetic uniqueness of various populations of muskellunge (MN, MO, ONT, WI). One study in Ontario has suggested that rather than having one species of muskellunge which is highly variable from area to area, there may be two species. While much more research of this type is needed before the final word is out on multiple species, the Ontario study does open the eyes of the muskellunge fraternity and poses interesting management concerns to biologists.

• Culture and stocking — Over the past century, artificial propagation and stocking of muskellunge has probably been the area of most muskellunge research. Early work concentrated on hatching success and stocking of fry, while work in the past several decades has been targeted more toward cost-effective rearing and stocking procedures. Recent research has dealt with various rearing techniques, many directed toward developing a more cost-effective stocking program. Some states (IL, NY, OH) are investigating the value of a dry diet vs. a minnow diet in rearing fish, or pond vs. trough-reared fish (OH). Typically, fish reared on dry diets are less expensive per fish, though survival can be lower compared to minnow-reared fish. Additional factors which are associated with post-stocking survival are also among current research topics. Understanding behavior patterns of muskellunge after stocking has helped to determine when and why fish are most vulnerable to predators after stocking (IL, OH, WI). One study (WI) found that fingerling muskellunge lack any avoidance behavior for the first several days following stocking, making them vulnerable to predators. Other studies (OH, IL) have documented that smaller stocked fish are more vulnerable to predators than larger ones.

A more recent area of interest in the area of muskellunge culture/stocking has been consideration of different genetic strains. Hatcheries are now becoming more aware of the importance of selecting brood stock for egg collections which are compatible with the native watershed to be stocked rather than other characteristics which may have only superficial value to the fishery such has high survival in rearing ponds.

• Harvest and exploitation — Overharvest of muskellunge has been a concern of biologists and muskellunge anglers for some time. In the past decade, muskellunge anglers practicing catch-and-release have contributed largely to improving the sport fishery in the face of increasing pressure. Nevertheless with the natural low abundances in which muskellunge occur, harvest can still be too high in some areas.

Determining actual harvest of muskellunge for a given water is troublesome compared to other sport fishes. If a muskellunge angler catches a fish of legal size he or she either releases it or leaves the lake immediately (most areas have a one-bag limit for muskellunge). Hence, unless the creel clerk is at the landing when the fish comes in, it will be missed in the survey.

Alternatives have been tested for determining muskellunge catch and harvest. Voluntary registration boards posted at resorts and taverns on muskellunge waters allow anglers the opportunity to voluntarily register fish. Research (WI) has shown that these boards have a tendency to underestimate actual harvest, though their success is quite variable from lake to lake. Explanations for this include the failure to register smaller, legal-sized fish and the secretive nature of some muskellunge anglers.

Another method recently being researched (MN, OH, ONT) has been the use of a voluntary reporting system. Under this format, anglers are given diaries to log in their fishing time and catch. The angler diary system seems promising for determining certain statistics on the muskellunge fishery, but needs continued involvement and support from angler groups. One apparent success story with voluntary reporting has been the Ohio Huskie Muskie Club. The Huskie Muskie Club requires pertinent information on catches (including a scale sample) to be reported for special recognition at the season's end.

Size limit regulations can protect fish under a given size. Current size limits for muskellunge are quite variable over the fish's range for a variety of biological and social reasons (see the chapter on Modern Management in this book). However, the effects of basic size limit changes on muskellunge populations are not well documented. Research studies designed to test the effects of size limits are in progress (WI) but more are needed.

Advocates of high size limits argue that no fish should be kept unless it is a trophy, while those against point out that catch and release is, in fact, producing a self-imposed size limit. Research (WI) on the social aspects of muskellunge fishing is an integral part of this and has helped define such vague areas as "what is a trophy."

• Life History — Determining basic life history characteristics of muskellunge may seem trivial, but in fact these studies form the foundation for any sound management program. Determining basic population abundance, growth and food habits information of a muskellunge population is a difficult task but can lead to new understanding of the muskellunge. An example of this research deals with the problems of accurately determining the age of large muskellunge. Research on aging procedures (ONT) has suggested that a bone (cleithra) found just behind the gill flap of a muskellunge provides the most accurate way to determine a fish's age. This holds true on older fish which may reach ages of over 25 years. Because cleithra bones cannot be collected unless a fish is dead, much of the collection is done by taxidermists. Taxidermists throughout the range of the muskellunge are requested to send cleithra bones from trophy fish they receive for mounting to Ontario researchers where they are aged.

Another new study (WI) is determining how the diet of muskellunge can affect other gamefish populations. In some regions, concerned sport anglers feel muskellunge eat too many other gamefish, such as walleyes. This study hopes to shed some light into muskellunge food habits and the impact these large predators might have on other fisheries.

We have identified the components required to conduct a research study, and outlined current muskellunge research. What should the future direction of muskellunge research be? What are priorities for research?

Priorities for new research projects need to be carefully thought through by all involved. This could mean peer review of a research proposal, or it could involve input of active muskellunge angler groups. For example, the Esocid Technical Committee mentioned above offers an excellent forum for review of new research ideas. In addition, angler groups such as Muskies, Inc., have their own research committees to promote and assist muskellunge research. This type of involvement fosters the sharing of ideas and enhances the chances of a successful research study.

Research priorities for the future should include further work in many of the above mentioned topics. Research on muskellunge habitat requirements at various life stages along with work targeted toward the rehabilitation of degraded habitat remain at the top of the list. Also among top priorities are determining the importance of different genetic strains of muskellunge and the impact of introducing non-native strains on resident populations. Stocking and culture of muskellunge will remain key management tools in certain regions, however the focus may shift toward cost-effective stocking strategies and rearing of native strains.

The final, but not the least important, topic remains the basic research directed toward life history of muskellunge. Already the use of cleithra bones has opened many eyes to the potential longevity of a muskellunge; earlier aging techniques did not reveal the full potential life span.

As we move closer into the next century, the status of the muskellunge resource remains in the hands of concerned anglers and biologists. In their aquatic world, adult muskellunge live at the top of the food chain with few natural enemies. It seems somewhat ironic a fish that can reach such large size and prominence in its domain is so vulnerable to the advancements of man and society. A solid research agenda along with continued involvement from the anglers who love this fish so dearly offer a guiding light for the future of the muskellunge.

MODERN MANAGEMENT

Is the musky really the "fish of 10,000 casts?" Which lakes harbor the really big muskies? Is there a new world record musky out there somewhere? Why don't we see any truly monstrous muskies anymore?

These commonly-asked questions attest to the fact that the musky is regarded as a "trophy" fish to nearly all who pursue it these days. Most muskies that are kept end up at the taxidermist's shop. Few are those anglers who regard muskies as a food fish. However, angler's definitions of a trophy musky vary widely.

The challenge for fisheries managers today is to protect the muskellunge fishery while attempting to shorten the time between hits and still provide opportunities for anglers with very different expectations from the fishery; not an easy task by any means.

One of the most significant changes in today's musky fishing has been the increasing popularity of the catch and release ethic. It used to be that you didn't have a successful day unless you had your picture taken with a musky hanging on the hook at the local baitshop. Many of today's musky anglers have a better understanding of the limitations of musky populations. They realize that a fish which can live to be over 30 years old is not easily replaced. Who but a musky angler could describe a successful outing by saying, "No, I didn't catch any, BUT I saw one!"

Most of the credit for the popularity of catch and release is due to organized musky angling groups such as Muskies, Inc., and numerous local clubs. Release rates among these anglers are commonly as high as 97 percent. These groups have also taken an active role in working with resource agencies, even providing funding for research and management efforts.

The key to the success of catch and release is proper handling and release techniques which give the musky the best chance for survival. Chief among these are minimizing landing and handling time, cutting deeply-embedded hooks, and support of the musky's body to prevent internal injury. All of this is best done without removing the musky from the water. Does it work? You bet it does. Recapture by anglers of tagged muskies has documented good survival. Muskies, Inc.,

catch records show one musky was even caught and released five times. Education in proper release methods is crucial. Organized musky angling groups have led the way in this effort.

Musky fishing tournaments have also become a big part of the musky fishing scene, particularly during the fall. Tournaments are conducted by numerous organizations including musky clubs, chambers of commerce and resorts. Some are season-long events while others are weekend outings. Most tournaments are strictly catch and release and, with proper release procedures, result in very few dead fish. Tournament fishing has its opponents who express concerns ranging from damage to the resource if many fish are kept or die after release, to increased boat traffic and noise on the water. Many state and provincial resource agencies require formal permitting procedures for tournaments which, if administered properly, will reduce both the biological and social concerns associated with musky fishing tournaments.

So how good is musky fishing these days? The most unbiased approach for measuring angler success is through a random, stratified, on-water angler survey also known as a creel survey. This complicated-sounding survey involves a survey clerk on the water counting anglers and interviewing them about their fishing success during randomly selected times throughout the fishing season. From this known information, accurate projections of fishing success can also be made for the times when the clerk is not present.

Creel surveys conducted by the Wisconsin Department of Natural Resources (WDNR) in northern Wisconsin indicate that it currently takes an angler fishing specifically for muskies an average of 20 hours to catch one. Still, unless you can make about 10 casts per minute, it's much better than "the fish of 10,000 casts".

Creel surveys also provide estimates of angler harvest. Estimates of musky harvest are difficult since few are actually measured by the creel survey clerk. Alternative means of measuring harvest are records from clubs and resorts. These records generally underestimate harvest since not all anglers participate and smaller, legal-sized fish are often not reported. Complete angler diaries are presently being tested. Tag returns can also provide a minimum estimate of musky harvest. Both resource agencies and organized angling groups like Muskies, Inc., are conducting tagging studies.

Despite the difficulty in measuring musky harvest, available information indicates that it currently does not exceed levels which would lead to overall declines in musky fisheries. In fact, overall numbers of muskies in Wisconsin lakes have likely increased since the 1960s and '70s. However, a concern is that selective angling harvest has resulted in fewer really big fish than in the past.

Results from a 1990 WDNR mail-in survey suggests that about 25,000 anglers regularly pursue muskies in Wisconsin. That's a lot of anglers to spread out over roughly 700 musky lakes in the state. When asked how they chose specific lakes to fish, most responded that a chance to catch a "big" (trophy) fish was of primary importance. Nearly all said that a trophy musky would be at least 40 inches long; the most common answer was 50 inches. The second most important reason for lake selection was aesthetics, a quality experience on a natural-looking lake. The biggest concern expressed by these anglers for the future of musky fishing was tribal harvest.

Tribal harvest by Chippewa Indians became a factor in musky management in Wisconsin in 1983 with the reaffirmation in federal court of off-reservation treaty harvest rights. The harvest currently has two primary components, spring open water spearing and winter spearing through the ice. The spring spearing harvest is tightly controlled by a quota system and complete harvest monitoring. Winter ice spearing is controlled by a daily bag limit and voluntary reporting. Any size musky may be speared. Tribal harvest of musky has generated considerable controversy raising concerns such as spear wounding rates, spearing of trophy-sized fish, and lack of quotas for ice spearing. Impacts of spearing on musky populations are not yet fully known. In any case, spearing remains an additional harvest element that must be accounted for in managing musky populations.

There are more musky anglers now than back in the "good old days." They also carry with them a much wider array of sophisticated gear and angling techniques than ever before. Despite a high release rate, these anglers harvest a considerable number of muskies. There is also an additional element of tribal harvest.

Fisheries biologists are continually monitoring the effects that all harvest is having on musky populations throughout North America. They look for changes in abundance, sizes, growth rates, and reproductive success. These factors indicate the relative health of musky populations and the need for management efforts to sustain the fishery.

Change in abundance is perhaps the most difficult factor to measure. Since fish in a lake can't simply be counted like trees on a piece of land, numbers must be estimated. The most intensive and accurate method is a mark-recapture population estimate. These estimates are usually conducted in the early spring when adult muskies congregate in the shallows for spawning. Muskies are usually captured with large trap nets called fyke nets set in spawning areas. Muskies swimming along the shoreline encounter the net and are funneled into the trap end. Netting surveys generate plenty of interest from people who come out to observe the process. It's exciting to see a net full of thrashing muskies which often prompts the question, "How do you get a job like that?" That question is rarely asked, however, on the frequent days when it's snowing and equipment is freezing solid.

Muskies captured in the fyke nets are measured, sex is determined, scale samples are taken for age determination, and the fish are "marked" permanently using either a numbered tag or by clipping off a fin. After allowing sufficient time for these "marked" fish to mix with the rest of the muskies in the lake, a "recapture" sample is taken. The number of muskies in the lake is then calculated based on the percentage of previously "marked" musky in the "recapture" sample. Long experience by fisheries biologists worldwide has shown the mark-recapture method to be a reliable means of estimating fish abundance.

Estimates in northern Wisconsin through 1994 show that musky populations have, on average, one adult musky for every two acres of water. Of these adult fish, about 10 percent are longer than 40 inches and only one-tenth of one percent are longer than 50 inches. To put this in perspective, if your favorite musky lake is 1,000 acres in size, then there are probably about 500 adult muskies in it but only 50 are longer than 40 inches and only one is over 50 inches.

That's not very many big fish!

While less comprehensive than actual population estimates, catch records from less intensive netting surveys and long-term complete angler catch records where available provide useful information in tracking changes in relative abundance and sizes of muskies in a lake over time.

Radio telemetry is also being used to determine movements and habitat use by muskies. Muskies are implanted with a small transmitter which allows fisheries biologists to track their movements. These studies have management application in identification of critical spawning habitats and other areas in lakes important to muskies at different times of the year.

Juvenile, or young, muskies are not easily sampled using the fyke nets

Muskies captured by fish biologists are measured and often weighed, as seen above. The sex is determined, scale samples are taken, and the fish are "marked" — either tagged or have a fin-clipped. Preceding page — a large musky is removed from a fyke net.

which are so effective in capturing spawning adults. Juvenile abundance is most often determined by sampling along shorelines at night in the fall with an electroshocking boat. The electric current produced by a generator temporarily stuns the young muskies long enough to be picked up by the crew. Although mark-recapture estimates are possible, most surveys provide indexes of abundance based on the numbers of young muskies caught per mile of shoreline electroshocked. These surveys are used to measure the success of natural reproduction or the survival of stocked muskies.

Surveys show that life is pretty tough out there if you're a young musky. Fewer than one percent of those that hatch from eggs will ever see adulthood. Competition from northern pike is one of many factors affecting early survival of muskies in some lakes. Northern pike often spawn in the same areas as muskies but do so several weeks earlier. Newly-hatched muskies are perfect food for the larger young northerns. Since muskies often select shallow bays with soft bottom substrate, egg hatching is often limited by physical factors such as sedimentation. Boat traffic can be a major cause of increased sedimentation. Loss of spawning areas due to shoreline development has become an increasing concern on many musky waters as lake residents "clean up" their shorelines.

Scales are removed from muskies captured for study to determine their age and growth rates.

Protection of spawning areas is critical to help maintain natural reproduction of muskies in the face of increasing lake use and development. The value of wild or undisturbed shorelines goes well beyond aesthetics.

Fisheries managers are increasingly examining the role muskies play in the entire fish communities of lakes. Diet studies provide insight into what muskies feed on at various life stages and at different times of the year. Population estimates of other fish species in addition to those for musky reveal trends in community composition.

Documentation of changes in physical habitat may provide answers to account for some changes in musky populations. This type of comprehensive approach to surveys gives a far better picture of the needs for management to maintain not only musky populations but other game and non-game fishes as well. The problem with comprehensive surveys is that they take considerable amounts of time and money. This is a problem for many resource agencies which have limited staffing to cover a multitude of lakes.

Just how well are musky populations holding up? Despite all the pressure from both man and nature, it is probably easier to catch a musky now than at any time in history. Fishery managers are unsure what "optimum" musky densities should be, but most anglers have few complaints about availability. The biggest concern today is not with the number of muskies but how big they are.

Growth rates for muskies are often determined by looking at scales taken from individual fish collected during survey work. Scales have growth rings called annuli which correspond to each year in the life of the fish. These annuli can be seen and counted when the scale is magnified. This method is very similar to aging trees by counting the growth rings. Muskies can be aged quite accurately using scales during the first 10 or so years of life. During these years growth is fairly rapid and annuli are quite distinct. Older muskies are more accurately aged by counting the annuli on the cleithrum (collar) bone. Most cleithrum aging information comes from angler-harvested fish since the musky must be killed in order to remove the cleithrum.

Growth rates of muskies vary considerably between lakes due to a combination of genetics, diet, and even lake type. Females also grow faster than males. However, in northern Wisconsin, it takes most muskies at least nine or 10 years to reach 40 inches in length. Information on growth rates is particularly important to fisheries managers for setting and evaluating size limits.

Harvest pressure and poor natural reproduction in many musky populations in Wisconsin as well as other Midwestern states has made stocking necessary to maintain many of these fisheries. Ontario, which contains most of Canada's musky water, does not have a hatchery program, however. Its fishery is totally dependent on natural reproduction.

Ideally, managing for naturally-reproducing populations is preferable to stocking. Expanding emphasis on genetic studies with muskies and other fish species throughout North America is reinforcing what is intuitively apparent. Physical separation over thousands of years has lead to measurable genetic differences between fish of the same species from different regions. Fish native to particular waters also generally display better growth, better survival, and more successful natural reproduction than fish from other regions. These genetic and behavioral differences are more pronounced between fish from widely separated locations.

The implication for stocking is that if stocked fish successfully reproduce with native fish, some genetic integrity is permanently lost which may lead to less fitness for survival in a particular lake. On the other hand, stocked fish may contribute desirable qualities such as better growth.

Resource agencies are increasingly concentrating on strain management. Lakes chosen by hatchery managers as egg sources from wild fish are more carefully selected for faster growing strains and close proximity to receiving waters. Minnesota has completely refocused its hatchery program with these factors in mind.

Many of Wisconsin's best musky waters receive at least some stocking. Less than 25 percent of these populations are considered totally naturally self-sustaining. This is quite the opposite situation from that of most other fish species, including walleye, in which the majority of populations are adequately supported by natural reproduction.

Wisconsin's musky stocking program is successful due to the high quality of the hatchery-reared fish. Many are nearly a foot long when stocked in the fall as young-of-the-year (fingerlings). These fish are larger than most wild fish of the same age. Survival following stocking is good in most lakes. Wisconsin currently stocks up to two of these large fingerlings per acre on an alternate year basis in lakes which require stocking.

Anglers should not underestimate the value of stocked muskellunge. At a production cost of over $2 per fish in Wisconsin, a stocked musky can be worth several thousand dollars to the fishery at maturity. This is because, as with naturally reproduced fish, most are eaten by predators or die of other causes before reaching adulthood.

Stocking will likely continue to be important to the overall management of muskies in many waters. Research suggests, however, that larger muskies may be more successful spawners than smaller fish. Greater numbers of large adults may improve natural reproduction. If more large muskies could be left in the waters through restrictive harvest regulations or voluntary release, there may be less need for stocking in the future. Protection and possibly rehabilitation of spawning areas is also needed.

Musky "catching" may be better now than ever before. There is little question that there are fewer really big muskies out there than in the past. Forty-pounders are very rare, and while large, they are a long way from the world record. Why are large muskies so scarce in most lakes? We know that some lakes with very slow growth rates do not have the potential to produce really big muskies but these are the exception rather than the rule. The biggest reason for the lack of big muskies is simple — harvest.

Muskies are trophy fish and the bigger they are, the greater is the likelihood that an angler will keep it. Even a 30-inch long musky is a trophy to many anglers. Creel surveys by the WDNR in northern Wisconsin from 1986-1990 revealed that half of all muskies harvested by anglers were less than 36 inches long and 78 percent of all those harvested were less than 40 inches. Records of 596 angler-caught muskies registered during 1989 in Wisconsin's Vilas County Musky Marathon were similar; 31 percent of the muskies kept were less than 36 inches long and 59 percent were less than 40 inches.

Aging information shows that 40-pound muskies are often over 20 years old. The 60-plus-pounders of record fame were never aged, but they may well have been over 30 years old. Despite the popularity of catch and release, the odds of a musky surviving that amount of time without being harvested is remote indeed.

Angling regulations for muskies in Wisconsin in 1935 stipulated a minimum size limit of 30 inches and a daily bag limit of one. Except for a small increase in the minimum size limit to 32 inches in 1983, Wisconsin's musky angling regulations remained virtually unchanged until 1990 despite obvious increases in angling pressure.

Muskies have always been considered trophy fish, and the larger they grow, the greater the likelihood of them being kept by anglers.

All of this has recently begun to change in Wisconsin as well as other states and Ontario, and at a rapid pace. Wisconsin now has a 34-inch minimum size limit statewide with exceptions including a 40-inch minimum size limit on 57 waters and a 45-inch minimum size limit on two waters. And, in Sawyer County, anglers are pushing for a 50-inch limit on select lakes. The state of Michigan adopted a 40-inch minimum size limit statewide in 1992; Minnesota followed in 1993. The province of Ontario maintains a 40-inch minimum size limit on most of its musky waters. Exceptions are a 34-inch minimum size limit on several waters with slow growth of muskies. Seven premier musky lakes in Ontario have a 48-inch minimum size limit for musky. One lake has a 52-inch minimum size limit and a few are currently catch and release only. Daily bag limits for all of these states and Ontario are one musky per day.

The need to protect or restore the numbers of truly big muskies has been the driving force behind higher size limits. The concern is shared by resource management agencies, anglers and many businesses dependent on quality musky fisheries. The very high size limits on some musky waters in Ontario, for instance, were asked for and supported by anglers and particularly resort interests in the province.

The rapid development of restrictive musky angling regulations is being accompanied by evalua-tions of the effect they will have on musky populations. Wisconsin has begun a 10-year study of the effects of a 40-inch size limit on northern Wisconsin musky populations. Changes in adult abundance, size structure, growth and reproduction are being monitored in 15 lakes of similar nature. Seven of these lakes have a 40-inch minimum size limit on muskies while eight have the current statewide 34-inch minimum size limit.

Indications are that angling regulations for muskies will continue to become more restrictive. Many anglers have expressed concerns regarding the need for further regulation changes including additional high size limits, season bag limits of one or two fish rather than a daily bag limit, and possibly gear restrictions. No single regulation will be applicable to all muskies fisheries as populations differ in growth rates and abundance. Social concerns including divergent angler attitudes and opinions will also shape musky regulations.

The future of the musky in North America is bright. Resource agencies are forging innovative and biologically-sound research and management efforts. They are finding support and input from an increasing number of concerned and dedicated musky anglers. With that kind of backing, the musky can't lose.

FOR THE RECORD

It has been said that the common name of the muskellunge originated from the Ojibwa dialect of *mas*, meaning ugly, and *kinonge*, meaning fish. Ever since the Indians' and fur trappers' and traders' earliest encounters with this finny beast, many stories and legends began to be told across the campfires and were chronicled by the first angler/explorer/writers of the time. An almost mystical aura was created regarding this great fish that immediately lent itself to the spinning of many tall tales and exaggerations.

Because the smaller, more abundant, gamefish were accessible, most Indian tribes didn't consider the muskellunge to be a primary food fish. But the white settlers viewed the muskellunge as a marketable commodity and subjected the species to sometimes heavy commercial fishing pressure between the time of the Civil War and the turn of the century. Recorded accounts of heavy commercial nettings in some Canadian lakes and the Great Lakes had, by 1900, muskellunge populations depleted to a point where commercial netting was no longer feasible. As muskellunge populations gradually began to rebound in those bodies of water, sport fishing began to grow.

During the 1880s, the waters of New York's St. Lawrence River and Lake Chautauqua became one of Musky Country's first hotbeds of muskellunge fishing as anxious Easterners flocked to these areas in search of old esox. But during this same time period about 800 miles to the west, in northern Wisconsin, sportfishing for the muskellunge was beginning to take even deeper root. With the close of the logging era around 1900 in

Preceding pages — Taxidermists Ron (left) and Rick Lax hold the mounts of the two largest tiger muskies ever caught. Ron holds Delores Ott Lapp's 50-pound 4-ounce fish from 1951, and Rick holds John A. Knobla's 51-pound 3-ounce fish from 1919. Ron Lax has recently remounted both muskies.

that region, the seeds were planted for the development of an extensive resort and tourism industry which eventually established northern Wisconsin as North America's premier musky fishing region.

As the great pineries of Wisconsin's north country became cleaned out, accommodations known as "stopping places" began to cater less to loggers and teamsters and more to fishermen and other outdoor enthusiasts. These often remote stopping places became Wisconsin's first "resorts." In the towns, hotels and boarding houses began to cater to these early tourists as well. Although private rooms were available to the more affluent, bunks were the norm. These rudimentary accommodations offered little luxury and attracted few females. A common practice for these early "musky men" was to troll spoons from birch bark canoes or from loggers' bateaux. Occasionally, an angler would write about his exploits with exciting — and often exaggerated — accounts. After 1910, these accounts began to be more readily published in various outdoor magazines. This helped fuel and build up the musky mystique.

Many of these early tourists longed for the tremendous fishing opportunities and solitude and isolation that the peaceful wilderness of northern Wisconsin had to offer. They endured long, hard journeys on their northerly treks. Just as the stopping places began catering more to sportsmen as logging began to die off, so did the railroad. Instead of hauling logs, they began to haul passengers. Until after the 1920s, when serious road improvements began to occur, the railroad provided the only reliable transportation into Musky Country and the remote areas of northern Wisconsin and the Canadian wilderness.

Railroads regularly ran publicity ads boasting of the north country's great fishing and healthful air. Although the Canadian National Railway reached many of Canada's remote lakes (of which Lake of the Woods was the most publicized), Wisconsin, being more convenient and accessible to the masses, quickly became established as a musky mecca. The Soo Line, Chicago and North Western Railway, and Northern Pacific Railway made many of Wisconsin's and Minnesota's prime musky waters accessible. Fishermen were met by livery at various stops and then carted off to their resorts. The first passenger train

One of the first resorts built on Wisconsin's famous Chippewa Flowage was Lessard's Resort, seen about 1925.

service into Minocqua, Wisconsin, began in January of 1888. By 1900, excursion trains such as the much publicized "Fisherman's Special" had become popular, making weekend runs from Chicago, through Milwaukee, and north to Star Lake, Wisconsin.

Those who dared travel north by wagon or auto during the first two decades of the 1900s commonly found the tote roads and logging roads to be an endless series of mud pits and practically impassable after a heavy rain. It wasn't unheard of for these vehicles to drive on the railroad tracks, which provided a very firm, level, but sometimes dangerous riding surface. Those drivers needed to know the train schedules!

One musky fisherman, who chronicled his 1915 travel experiences of a musky trip to Round Lake, Wisconsin, in an *Outdoor Life* article, wrote:

"Our journey from the train station to the lake by auto reminded me of trips I have taken in an areoplane and submarine. When not sailing through the air we were plowing through mud and water."

When this author finally reached his destination, a camp isolated on a bluff overlooking a beautiful body of water, he was taken aback by how the remoteness of his locale so contradicted the destruction man had wroth on such a virgin land. He wrote:

"It presented anything but a prepossessing picture. A few trees alone presented a slight semblance of the beauty and grandeur that one would expect close to the bosom of Nature. The once primeval forest in proximity to it had been cut down by lumbermen years ago and devastation by fire had done the rest. We are so inured to such conditions in our quest for good fishing that we try not to let it ruffle our equanimity."

Newly created resorts, offering more comfortable and exclusive accommodations, began to be built in Wisconsin during the 1880s and 1890s to cater to tourists and fishermen. Two of the earliest known resorts in the Minocqua/Woodruff area were a resort that Frank Roemer operated on Big St. Germain Lake during the mid 1880s and Ed Walsh's resort, built on Lake Shishebogama in 1896. Two other early resorts of that area were Hanson's Squirrel Lake Resort and Shorewood Lodge, both on Squirrel Lake. In the Hayward area, where by the mid 1880s numerous stopping places were already beginning to accommodate "hook and line enthusiasts," a man named Jacob Christie is credited as the first person to build a resort for fishermen. Built in 1885 a quarter mile from Spider Lake, Christie's resort was built perhaps a little bit ahead of its time. For with logging still in full bloom and with his resort being so far off the beaten path, his business really didn't become well established as a fishing resort until William Cornick took over the place in 1894. In 1888, Jericho Resort was built on Grindstone Lake near Hayward and, in 1890, a 90-room hotel was built in Cable, Wisconsin.

During this same period, wealthy fishermen formed exclusive fishing clubs which built large "clubhouses" or clusters of cottages on various Wisconsin lakes. In effect, these small groups of businessmen owned and vacationed on their own private "closed" resorts. Walter Cronkite's grandfather became a charter member of one such fishing club in 1906 — the Wismo Angling Club on Lac Courte Oreilles, Wisconsin.

With northern Wisconsin nestled right in the heart of prime Musky Country, it was inevitable for a boom-

Facing page — Early 20th century anglers show off their catch out of Sayner's Resort at Sayner, Wisconsin.

s Catch Of Muskellunge At Sayner's Resort, Sayner, Wisconsin

ing resort industry to sprout up after the lumbermen's axes were stilled. This industry that was generated over 100 years ago is still going strong today. No wonder the Wisconsin State Legislature officially declared the muskellunge Wisconsin's state fish in 1955.

With the number of published angling accounts on the increase and more people taking an interest in sportfishing, the establishment of a wide variety of accommodations for all would-be anglers, and increasing numbers of game fish being caught each year, came a time for the keeping of accurate angling records. In 1911, *Field & Stream* magazine met that demand by becoming the first organization to, on a national scale, record the great angling catches of each species. By instituting a highly publicized annual fishing contest program and awarding cash prizes for the largest entries of each species, *Field & Stream* encouraged the registration and permanent recording of scores of historic angling catches. In 1920, *Field & Stream* published its first world record listing of both fresh and salt water catches.

During the mid 1970s, at about the time when the task of continuing its fresh water records program was becoming too costly and time consuming for *Field & Stream*, a new organization was formed — solely to specialize in fresh water record keeping and to preserve, in a continually expanding museum, all aspects of the history of fresh water angling. This new organization, the National Fresh Water Fishing Hall of Fame (NFWFHF), continued *Field & Stream's* practice of recording all of the world's largest, legally caught, fresh water fish. Because of this policy of record keeping, the NFWFHF is actually the only organization to determine what "the" world record for each fresh water species is.

In 1978, when *Field & Stream* ceased keeping fresh water records, the International Game Fish Association (IGFA) took over the fresh water records program. Up until that point, the IGFA had been solely a salt water record keeper. The IGFA's record keeping policies differ slightly from *Field & Stream's* in that the IGFA does not record the largest fresh water fish of each species that has been legally caught by an angler; rather, it selectively records those fish which satisfy the club's requirements. Because of this fundamental policy difference, the IGFA is not always the determining organization to decide what "the" world record for each fresh water fish is. In most cases the IGFA world record is usually the same as "the" world record but, because their rules go beyond whether a fish has been legally caught, not every IGFA world record happens to be "the" world record. In those cases, the IGFA world record is merely its own club's listed world record.

Such is the case with the current world record

muskellunge of 69 pounds 11 ounces caught by Louis Spray out of Wisconsin's Chippewa Flowage back in 1949 — the largest known muskellunge catch of all time. Spray's musky, legally caught at the time of its catch, was shot in the water to be killed before being boated — a legal and recommended method used to subdue muskies in Wisconsin up until 1966. Naturally, being a legal catch, the NFWFHF (as well as *Field & Stream*, the record keeping predecessor) has declared Spray's musky to be the all tackle world record musky. Because the IGFA has a rule against accepting any fish that has been shot, it lists Cal Johnson's 67 1/2-pound musky, caught out of Wisconsin's Lac Court Oreilles in 1949, as its world record musky.

Soon after the formation of *Field & Stream's* annual fishing contest in 1911, entries began to pour in. The largest musky that was entered that year was a 48-pound, 59-inch fish caught by Dr. Frederick Whiting. Although it's very likely that some larger muskies had been caught prior to this one, there is no record of them and Dr. Whiting's musky is recognized as the first official world record musky. Whiting and his companion, Mr. Corbett, a veteran angler with an unrivaled string of musky kills to his credit, were equipped with what was state of the art gear when they made their capture on the St. Lawrence River. Whiting was row trolling a No. 9 Corbett spoon with a feathered three-gang hook, using a large brass swivel and three-foot copper leader,

a 7-foot-6 Von Lengerke and Detmold split bamboo rod, and No. 4 Vom Hofe reel with 300 feet of braided linen line.

While Dr. Whiting was fishing in the lap of luxury on the St. Lawrence, that same year, an 11-year-old lad — who couldn't afford to buy a rod and reel — captured a brute musky out of Butternut Lake, Wisconsin, that gave the Whiting fish a run for its money. The boy — accompanied by his friend, Miles Hamilton — borrowed a boat from a local farmer, George Stubblefield, to go fishing. Having no gear of

A rare, colorized photo of Louis Spray and his world record 69-pound 11-ounce musky caught in 1949.

his own in those days, the boy went into the woods and cut a strong tamarack pole to which he attached a length of yellow chalk line his father had given him. After catching a live frog and impaling it on a spoon hook the boys were in business. Working the lure behind the boat in a zig-zag fashion, the boy was terrified as a monster musky took the pole and all away from him. Later, upon returning to the scene with the farmer, the trio found the pole floating and, after a lengthy and exciting battle, captured a 46 1/2-pound, 55-inch musky!

Ironically, had this fish been entered and accepted into *Field & Stream's* fishing contest, it might have become the first world record musky ever recorded and this 11-year-old boy could have been the first to claim the title. By the way, that young Wisconsin lad's name was Louis Spray.

Today, with the 21st century upon us and during an age of high tech fishing gear and electronics, we often lose touch with the origins of our sport. Learning about the old musky ways enriches our perception of our early muskellunge heritage and helps keep alive the mystique of a wondrous sport.

Some of the old musky ways and tactics may seem a little ludicrous. During a July 1912 musky fishing trip to Teal Lake, Wisconsin, an angler chronicled his experiences in a subsequent *Outdoor Life* article. After their normal offerings of spoons tipped with frogs or pork didn't yield any musky action, the angler and his wife became inventive. He wrote:

"My wife suggested we use mice of which our cabin was full. I was skeptical about them, until she made a cast over a weed bed and started to reel. There was a swirl in the water as a musky snatched the lure. She finally brought the fish to gaff and it proved to be a fair sized one. We used mice a number of times thereafter and were successful. Later she suggested squirrels and the muskies took them also, but my suggestion that we try cats and dogs did not meet her approval. An angler once informed me that while duck shooting in fall he noticed that a duck he had killed was snatched from the surface of the water by a large musky. The next day he took out his fishing tackle and baited the hooks with a small duck and caught a musky!"

Another favorite livebait tactic was to put a live chipmunk, harnessed with treble hooks, onto a shingle or piece of wood. The line from the rod went to the shingle, which was connected to the chipmunk by a long leader. After placing the chipmunk on the shingle in a good musky haunt and the angler had quietly rowed some distance away, a sharp jerk with the rod tip put the "bait" into the water. What musky could refuse

Wisconsin guide Eddie Walters, circa 1940. Note the pistol and the bullet hole in the head of one heck of a big musky.

such a meal?!

The "musky spike" was a very crude method of using suckers as livebait. With a line tied to the center of a spike and the spike slid deep into a sucker's gullet, the sucker was then trolled behind a boat. Once hit and swallowed by a ravenous and unsuspecting musky, a hard hookset would lodge the spike crossways in the musky's gullet — obviously, not a good method to use on a musky that was to be released.

In Wisconsin, until 1966, shooting muskies was a legal and often recommended method of killing a musky brought boatside after the fight. During the "old days," before there was any significant release program, people rarely found it necessary to handle muskies alive. Because of a musky's comparatively large head and ominous looking set of jaws, most people had an understandable fear of handling a live musky. So, before handling a large musky and bringing it into the boat, the logical thing was to first kill the fish in the water. Shooting muskies with a small caliber pistol seemed to be the most efficient way of accomplishing that task. Here are a few tried and true tips on shooting muskies from a master — Louis Spray:

"Always be sure that the fish's head is at least a little above the water before you shoot, and watch out for your line as it might be rolled around the fish in the process of fighting. You might shoot the line off. If you have a fish on and other boats move in to have a look, don't be afraid to ask them to move away. The bullet might glance off the water and pose a threat to the other fishermen. If you have no pistol, a .22 rifle is alright. If you have neither, be sure to take along a nice club, 30 to 36 inches long."

Spray recalled this hard luck story that happened to his friend, Alton Van Camp:

"Van was using a long cable leader and large sucker hook through a sucker's nose. When Van shot a musky that had swallowed his sucker, the bullet went through the top of the musky's head, hit the wire leader dead center, and separated it! He lost the fish."

Stories about overexcited anglers shooting live muskies in the bottom of their boats are common. There must have been a lot of leaky boats during those years! If properly done, shooting muskies was an efficient way of landing large muskies; it's still a good thing that method was outlawed. Imagine giving a loaded weapon to someone as potentially hysterical as a fisherman with a huge musky on the end of his line!

How big do muskies get? From 1911 to 1949 a string of nearly a dozen world record muskies proved that there always seemed to be a bigger musky out there — until Louis Spray's 69-pound 11-ounce fish permanently topped the list. The very first person to crack the 50-pound mark — and snatch the world record title away from Dr. Whiting — was F. J. Swint who, on September 13, 1916, caught a stocky 51-pounder while row trolling a No. 8 skinner spoon and live frog in Chief Lake, Wisconsin (now part of the famed Chippewa Flowage).

And then, on July 16, 1919 out of Lac Vieux Desert, John A. Knobla caught a fish just three ounces heavier — a 51-pound 3-ounce, 54-inch hybrid musky — and hung onto the world record title for 10 years. A 52 3/4-pound musky caught by E. A. Oberland on July 1, 1929 out of Vilas County, Wisconsin's, Pokegama Lake stayed in the world record spot for less than two months, when it was surpassed by the first of a string of world record muskies which were to be taken from Canada's Lake of the Woods during the following three seasons. These three Canadian world record muskies (Gordon Curtis' 53 3/4-pounder from 1929; Jack Collins' 56 1/2-pounder in 1931; and George Neimuth's 58 1/4-pounder in 1932) brought Lake of the Woods immediate premier musky status, making it the place to be during the 1930s.

After Percy Haver reported catching a 58-pound 14-

ounce musky out of Michigan's Lake St. Clair in June of 1939, *Field & Stream* accepted the fish and awarded Haver the world record musky title, one that was rather short lived. Less than a month later, Louis Spray earned the title by catching a 59 1/2-pound beauty out of Hayward, Wisconsin's, Grindstone Lake. Perhaps it's poetic justice that Haver's "world record" was overshadowed so quickly, because it has recently been discovered that his catch was an exaggerated claim and has been disqualified from the official listing of former world record muskies. After experiencing nearly three fishless seasons prior to his victory, Spray's accomplishment proved to be especially sweet. With the persistence that he was known for, Louis had stuck with his fishing and it eventually paid off.

Spray's reign as "musky king" proved to be equally short lived though, for on October 3 of that same year (1939) John Coleman caught the first recorded musky in excess of 60 pounds! Coleman, a novice angler, took his 60 1/2-pound world record musky from Canada's Eagle Lake. In July of 1940, Percy Haver stole back the world record title after claiming to have caught a 62 1/2-pound fish out of Lake St. Clair, Michigan. And the following month — not yet being aware of Haver's claim, Louis Spray did it again, catching a 61-pound 13-ounce monster out Wisconsin's Lac Court Oreilles.

Originally believing his musky to be a new world record, Spray had to be disappointed upon discovering that his fish was 11 ounces short of beating Haver's newly established world record. It's interesting to note that even though Haver's musky was accepted as the world record by *Field & Stream* and Spray's big musky was not officially listed as such at the time, deep down in his heart, Louis Spray always considered his near 62-pounder to be a world record. In fact, he even went so far as to make reference to this fish as being a world record by having the following inscription deeply etched into his tombstone: "Here Lies The Remains Of Louis Spray. Three Record Muskies In His Day." And you know what … he was right!

While Haver's musky had always been regarded as rather dubious, it wasn't until recently that this fish did indeed prove to be an exaggerated and falsified entry with *Field & Stream*. Amazingly, the damning proof against Haver's fish, although out in the open, remained unnoticed for some 55 years. On the very photograph of the mount of his fish is — if one looks closely enough — a wooden builder's ruler with its faint, but readable, increments revealing the musky had been exaggerated by nearly six inches in length.

Other photographs of this same fish also support the realization that this musky's size had been grossly exaggerated and it would have have lucky to have been in the 40-pound class. Haver's fish has now been disqualified from the official listing of former world record muskies.

Using hindsight, it's unfortunate that Louis Spray's 61-pound 13-ounce musky wasn't weighed until three days after it was caught. In all likelihood, when it was freshly caught, it probably would have been a little heavier than Haver's exaggerated 62 1/2-pound musky anyway. Spray, who was running a contest to guess the weight of his musky, put his fish on ice and displayed it for three days while hundreds of gawkers came to view and guess its weight. Since there was a cash prize being offered to the winner, the fish remained unweighed until the contest closed. When the time came to weigh and measure the fish, it was impeccably done by a committee of three of Hayward's most upstanding citizens. Over 600 people signed a ledger and recorded their guesses and, ironically, the average of all the guesses came out to be less than a half-pound off of the actual weight of Spray's musky. This ledger is currently in the NFWFHF's archives and stands as the longest known

Alois Hanser with the musky that he passed off as a 64 1/2-pounder. In actuality, the fish's weight was probably 20 pounds less.

list of witnesses serving to document the existence of any muskellunge.

In 1947, the world record title was again wrongfully awarded — this time to Alois Hanser, who claimed catching a 64 1/2-pound musky out of Wisconsin's Favil Lake (a 42-acre "pothole lake" that would be lucky to produce a fish half that size). While there is a question of whether this fish was taken by conventional means, it's the given dimensions of this musky which prove it to be an exaggerated claim. For anyone well acquainted with the weight/length/girth relationships of trophy muskies, a quick glance at the photo of this fish confirms that some chicanery took place. Having a documented length of 58 inches and girth of only 24 inches, it is simply beyond the realm of possibility for Hanser's fish (most likely a mid 40-pound fish) to have weighed anywhere near its reported 64 1/2-pound weight. Never recognizing this apparent exaggeration, *Field & Stream* accepted the fish as a world record. It has since been disqualified from the official world record listing.

1949 was the golden year in the history of musky fishing, producing two of the largest musky catches ever — Cal Johnson's 67 1/2-pound and Louis Spray's 69-pound 11-ounce world records. A veteran outdoor magazine writer, Cal Johnson caught his 60 1/4-inch musky on July 24 from Lac Court Oreilles, Wisconsin. Phil Johnson, who was in the boat with his father when Cal caught his fish, poignantly remembered the events that led to that fateful day:

"Several years earlier (around 1946) doctors told my father that he had a serious heart condition and had only months to live. Quitting his job and moving to the Hayward area, my father intended on spending his remaining time enjoying the outdoors in the area that he loved. Miraculously, he improved and defied his doctor's bleak prognosis. And three years later, in 1949, he caught his world record musky — on borrowed time."

Only three months after Johnson caught his fish, on October 20, Louis Spray nailed his 69-pound 11-ounce, 63 1/2-inch record musky in Wisconsin's Chippewa Flowage. Although a variety of wild stories questioning the legitimacy of the Spray musky have been concocted over the years, the Spray musky is very well documented and beyond reproach. This fish still stands as the current all tackle world record muskellunge.

Cal Johnson in a rare, colorized photo with his 60 1/4-inch, 67 1/2-pound musky which stood as the world record for about three months before Louis Spray caught his near 70-pounder.

Louis Spray briefly recalled the catching of his great fish in a 1972 radio interview:

"I knew he was there. I'd been after him for several years myself. Off and on we'd fish there for an hour or so and then go and try somewhere else; but we'd always come back to it several times a day. Once I hooked him with my harnessed sucker, I noticed he was heavier to handle and I had to use a certain amount of horse sense. I had my pistol at many times, ready to shoot, but couldn't do it as the wind was quite high. George Quentmeyer, the guide, was busy with the boat and he got quite perturbed at least once when he thought I should have shot. He couldn't see exactly my predicament. Finally I got him up again and couldn't shoot so it went on past and I heard BING, BING. George had shot the fish twice in rapid succession, in a very vital spot and he killed it. Ted Hagg, and I, and Quentmeyer had fished for this 'Chin Whiskered Charlie' — at that time it was our 19th day."

At the turn of the century, muskellunge fishermen in northeastern Wisconsin were claiming the presence of another "species" of musky in some of their region's lakes and rivers — especially those of which were drained by the upper Wisconsin River. This well-marked, vertically barred, fish was often called "tiger musky" for its obvious appearance.

Actually, they were not a "species" but a hybridization caused by a northern pike fertilizing muskellunge eggs. Although their normal spawning periods are usually separated by about 10 days, a late spring with sudden warming trends can cause an overlapping of the fishes' spawning periods. This phenomenon is common in the Lake Superior snow country of northeastern Wisconsin and possibly explains why this region has always been such a "hybrid hotbed."

Most hybrid musky/northern are conceived in this natural way, but hybrids were artificially produced as well. Hybrids planted from hatchery stock were often used as an infertile predator to diminish stunted panfish without upsetting the native fishery in a lake. James Nevin, a Wisconsin fisheries biologist, was one of the first to recognize the hybrid as a cross strain and not a separate species. He was artificially producing them as early as 1900 at the Woodruff Hatchery. It is not known to what extent these fish were planted, but several very large hybrids which were caught prior to 1920 could have indeed come from Mr. Nevin's early stockings.

A 41-pounder was taken from Lake Kawaguesaga, near Minocqua, Wisconsin, in 1919 by Charles Casey. The same year, J. A. Knobla caught his world record of 51 pounds 3 ounces from Lac Vieux Desert, a lake straddling the Michigan-Wisconsin border. And, back in 1916, Art Jackson caught a huge hybrid from Little

St. Germain Lake that weighed a reported 56 pounds. Although a clear photo of this fish exists, there is no known documentation confirming this fish's weight and this musky takes its place along with several other "could have been, should have been" records.

In 1929 the Chicago Museum of Natural Sciences acknowledged the "tiger" musky as a cross strain rather than a species. This was some 29 years after Mr. Nevin crossed them in his tanks at the Woodruff Hatchery and one year after George Barber caught a spectacular hybrid of 49 pounds from Pelican Lake in Oneida County in Wisconsin.

Unlike the dramatic progression of the muskellunge world record which worked its way upward, pound by pound, from 1911 to 1949, the world record for hybrid musky/northern was caught very early on. However, recognition wasn't to come its way until as recent as the late 1970s.

The establishment of a state of Wisconsin world record for the hybrid was not without its own dramatic moments. In the early 1970s, nearby states had a listing for record hybrids among their game fish records but Wisconsin had none. So in 1975, a committee of private citizens formed in the Milwaukee area to seek out the largest hybrid taken in Wisconsin. Four large hybrids were the object of the committee's efforts. They were the aforementioned fish taken by Barber and Knobla, a 48 1/2-pounder taken in 1943 from Vilas

County's Pickerel Lake, and a more recently caught 50-pound 4-ounce fish from 1951 from Lac Vieux Desert by Delores Lapp of Land O' Lakes, Wisconsin. The Jackson fish (reportedly 56 pounds) did not come to public attention until 1990.

The Lapp fish could have weighed a bit more. A magazine article, written closer to the time Mrs. Lapp caught her fish, said her musky was taken during the morning hours and was not weighed for *Field & Stream* until late in the afternoon. It said the fish was first weighed "dockside" at Bill Swartz's Resort (now Sunrise Lodge) at "52 or 52 1/2 pounds." The same scale is still in use today for the Vilas County Musky Marathon contest. Because Mr. Swartz had died prior to the re-examination of these records, his testimony couldn't be gathered. The resort, then under new ownership, was searched for a receipt or note documenting that weight in Mr. Swartz's handwriting — but none was ever found. Even handwriting on the wall of the shelter would have had some bearing on the record.

Knobla's fish, although well documented, was thought to be a hybrid but, at that time, photographic proof was lacking. While the committee was trying to ascertain the weights of the other three large hybrids in question, a letter was sent to the state of Wisconsin's DNR Fisheries Bureau to inform it of what the committee was doing and politely asking it to prepare to accept the committee's findings for the next published listing of Wisconsin state record fish. The state was already listing "splake" and "tiger trout," both hybrids, on its record list but for unknown reasons omitted the hybrid musky/northern — a far more common and popular fish.

The reply to the committee's letter was shocking. The committee's offer was rejected. When the state's letter was read aloud at the ensuing meeting of the committee, it was received with uproarious laughter. Evidently, the state employee who replied thought the state had the final say in the matter. The reply to the DNR's letter was far more terse, pointing out that fishery employees do not control the record lists. The committee was to continue its work, the matter of the hybrid record was settled, and the Wisconsin DNR was invited to use the findings of the committee if they so desired. It did.

In June of 1977, in a ceremony at the Sunrise Lodge on the shores of Lac Vieux Desert, Delores Ott Lapp, daughter of a resort owner and wife of a fishing guide, was presented with a plaque naming her fish as the state and world record for the hybrid muskellunge/northern pike.

Research on the Knobla fish continued and several years later Rod Ramsell of St. Paul, Minnesota, discovered a clear photo of the Knobla fish on microfilm in a library. The photo unmistakably proved the fish to be a hybrid. Upon displaying it to a majority of the hybrid committee, it was agreed the fish was a hybrid and since both the Lapp and Knobla fish were documented by the same organization (*Field & Stream* magazine), it was further agreed that the Knobla fish — documented as being 15 ounces heavier — should be considered the world record.

The mounts of both 50-pounders are on display in Land O' Lakes retail stores and can be viewed by the public. Both mounts have been remounted by Conover, Wisconsin, taxidermist Ron Lax — in both cases the results are impressive and these two great catches are well preserved for years to come. The Lapp fish, which was 56 inches in length and had a 26-inch girth, fell to a Marathon Musky Houn. The Knobla fish, which was 54 inches long fish with a 26 1/2-inch girth, was caught on a Skinner Spoon, the forerunner of today's bucktail.

Of the 21 known hybrids over 40 pounds, 20 were caught in Wisconsin. However, with its range greatly expanded and many legal catches being released, the probability of a catch over 52 pounds looms large in other U.S. and Canadian waters.

This next section, covering various hoaxes, legends, and "could have beens," will be headed by a brief explanation of the infamous Lawton musky. This musky, reportedly caught in 1957 in the St. Lawrence River by Art Lawton and thought to be 69 pounds 15 ounces, held the world record title for some

35 years. It was believed to be legitimate but, in 1992, was proven to be a falsified catch by musky historian John Dettloff. As a result, the Lawton musky was officially disqualified on August 6, 1992, in a joint decision issued by the NFWFHF and the IGFA. The true world record musky caught by Louis Spray was then again reinstated with its original world record status.

This landmark discovery that has so rocked the musky fishing community represents musky fishing's "crime of the century." Summing up the reason for the disqualification: precise mathematical calculations, taken off newly discovered photos of the Lawton musky, indisputably proved the Lawton fish to have been much smaller than claimed. (For details on all the facts on this matter, reference the October/November 1992 issue of *Musky Hunter* magazine or the December 1992 issue of *Outdoor Life*.)

As mentioned earlier in this chapter, because of all of the hysteria that usually goes along with the sport of musky fishing, stories of great musky sightings and catches have always been prone to exaggerations. Slight embellishments have always been commonplace and don't often raise many eyebrows. But when it comes to grossly falsifying contest winning or world record class musky catches, there is no room for lies.

During the past five years, the hallowed 50-pound-plus musky list has been undergoing careful scrutiny. The list has already experienced a major revision, changing the status quo by both reshaping our sport's written history and changing the way in which we assess the quality of our fisheries today. This historic listing of the world's greatest musky catches must be kept as accurate as possible — out of fairness to all of the fishermen who have made legitimate musky catches in excess of 45 pounds.

To date, 30 muskies (13 reportedly caught by Len and Betty Hartman, 12 reportedly caught by Art and Ruth Lawton, four reportedly caught by Percy Haver, and one reportedly caught by Alois Hanser) originally claimed to have been over 50 pounds have been officially disqualified by Larry Ramsell, fish historian for the NFWFHF. Fourteen of these fish were originally claimed to have been over 60 pounds and three were listed as world records.

For years, these bogus catches provided us with false benchmarks by which all legitimate trophy muskies have been compared to. We now know that huge muskies have always been more rare than we were all originally led to believe and that, in reality, only six or seven 60-pound-plus muskies and around two dozen 55-pound-plus muskies have ever been caught.

A few "could have beens," muskies that didn't quite make the grade to become world records, are worth mentioning. The Malo musky, a huge musky that was never accurately weighed (but possibly in the 70-pound class), was reportedly caught in the spring of 1954 by

Robert Malo in Middle Eau Claire Lake in Wisconsin. The mount of this fish, impressive and well preserved, is currently on display at the Dun Rovin Lodge near Hayward. While this fish is undoubtedly huge, its exact weight is uncertain. It was weighed first on an uncertified scale and a second time on a certified scale — but after the taxidermist had begun to cut into the fish.

Another huge musky, captured by noted guide Allison Drake (circa 1924) below the Moose Lake Dam on the West Fork of the Chippewa River in Wisconsin, if properly weighed and registered with *Field & Stream*, could have been declared a world record. It was said to have bottomed out a 50-pound scale, weighing a reported 56 pounds. Judging from the photo of this very impressive fish, we have no arguments — for the fish appears to be a heavy, 55 -inch class fish. The accepted world record musky at the time was 51 pounds 3 ounces.

The catching of a Canadian French River monster musky in 1947 before the season opened made some angler the victim of bad timing. This fish, reportedly 68 pounds 14 ounces, 62 1/4 inches long, and with a thick 35 3/4-inch girth, was promptly confiscated by conservation officials and couldn't be considered for world record status. The fish was mounted and publicly displayed until it mysteriously vanished after the building it was displayed in was remodeled.

There are numerous stories of captures — whether by hook and line, net, or by other means — of 60- to 100-pound class muskies during various times in our history. Quite often, the age of the story seems to be directly proportional to the amount of exaggeration that occurred. One such musky was netted in Lake Michigan during the mid 1800s, reportedly weighing 162 pounds. The skull of this musky was preserved, measured, and compared with the heads of other muskies of known size. The dimensions of this "mystery skull" turn out to be more consistent with that of a musky in the 45- to 50-pound class.

The famous 1902 nettings of two huge muskies, reportedly a 102-pounder from Lake Minocqua and an 80-pounder from Lake Tomahawk, was a well known event. These fish were being stripped of their spawn and then were returned to the water by E. D. Kennedy. According to his son, the legendary guide Jim Kennedy, "Perhaps the story is true, but the whiskey flowed quite freely in those days." In 1925, while researching the story, Cal Johnson found out that those fish never were weighed — but were estimated.

Art and Ruth Lawton stand behind one week's catch in September 1957. The fourth musky from the right is the one Art passed off as a 69-pound 15-ounce world record, but later discovered to be a 49 1/2-pound 55-incher. The Lawton "world record" was disqualified in 1992.

A 1923 newspaper account told about the discovery of a huge musky found dead in Lake Tomahawk, Wisconsin. They seemed to "lay it on a little thick" as well, reporting the musky to be 78 pounds, 59 inches long with a 25 1/2-inch girth, six inches between the eyes, have a jaw spread of 13 1/2 inches, and have a tail that fanned open to 15 inches. Two wooden lures, 12 spoon hooks, 18 pike hooks, and a three-pound pike were supposedly found inside the fish. Well, with all that "metal" inside the fish, no wonder it made 78

The Minocqua Times dutifully reported the alleged capture of 102-pound and 80-pound muskies by Wisconsin Conservation Department officials in 1902.

LARGEST MUSKALLONGE EVER CAPTURED!

Supt. Nevin of the State Fish Hatchery Commissioners, who has been taking muskallonge spawn at the Tomahawk and Minocqua lakes the past month, informes us that E. D. Kennedy and himself captured the two largest muskallonge ever taken in these waters. The largest one was caught in Minocqua lake, and weighed 102 pounds, the other being taken in Tomahawk lake and weighed 80 pounds. After the spawn was taken from these monsters they were turned back into their native waters, where they await the sportsman to try and land them. Mr. Nevin has taken muskallonge spawn at this place for the past four years, and says that in seining this season they have caught more small muskallonge than ever before, which goes to show that they are increasing. He also informes us that they have about 25,000,000 pike fry ready for distribution, and 2,000,000 muskallonge fry, which will be planted in the lakes of Vilas, Oneida and Forest counties. The State Fish Hatcher Commissioners are expected here Saturday to look over the hatchery at this place and to lay out improvements to be done.

pounds! This musky was most likely in the 50- to 55-pound class and had died of old age. These kind of tales are all pretty harmless but in those who believe them, an unrealistic perspective can develop.

Tales of captures and sightings of 80- to 100-pound and six- and seven-foot muskies are not restricted to the past, either. As long as old esox continues to patrol the waters of Musky Country don't expect these stories to stop — it's part of the mystique of our sport.

In 1987, the Wisconsin DNR shocked a massive musky in Lake Wissota that fueled many anglers' hopes of catching a new world record. Most rumored DNR nettings of 80- to 100-pound muskies are just that — rumor and nothing more. But this event, well documented and witnessed by two experienced fisheries men, was different — it really occurred. The only question is, how big was the fish? Reports had the fish ranging from six to eight feet long and up to 100 pounds. Although the reports were very generous, the fish could have been of world record class! The musky was never handled by the two men, it just momentarily surfaced near their boom shocking boat and, after a quick estimate of six feet in length was made, the musky disappeared into the murky depths. Even if their estimate was a little off, we are still talking about a huge fish — one at least in the mid 50-pound range and maybe of record class.

In 1983, a Wisconsin newspaper headline read, "7-Foot Fish Bares Teeth In Wisconsin" after a 13-year-old swimmer was attacked by a large musky in Island Lake, near Rhinelander. The attack caused the young girl to require 15 stitches in her foot and scared most of the other swimmers off the lake for a while. Of course, it did attract quite a few fishermen! Although the girl's wounds were certainly not imagined, the seven-foot estimate does seem a bit dramatic.

Are world record class muskies alive today? You bet! Just ask Toronto angler Ken O'Brien who, in 1988, caught a whopping 65-pound near record musky out of Canada's Georgian Bay. This fish not only spurred on the musky world's enthusiasm of the prospect of a new world record musky being caught, but also proves that any of us has a bona fide chance at someday catching a new world record. For this was O'Brien's first musky and he was walleye fishing at the time. Here's his personal account of that day:

"It was a beautiful fall day with the leaves at their peak as two friends and myself began trolling for walleye in Georgian Bay's Blackstone Harbor. We usually troll the edges of the harbor which is kind of like a small lake. When I caught the big one, I was using a small, silver, four-inch countdown Rapala. To troll it a little deeper, I had added a few split shots in front of the lure. After cutting a corner a bit too close, my partners' lures hooked weeds and then mine did too — or at least I thought it did. Quickly discovering what was on the end of my line was really a whale of a musky, I couldn't believe it! Surprisingly, it was an anticlimactic fight. The fish moved slowly, but with power, and I thought as soon as this musky 'wakes up,' it would be all over. But it never did anything spectacular and within only 10 or 15 minutes, we hauled it into the boat. I knew the musky was big (perhaps 45 or 50 pounds), but had no idea what I really had. Upon returning to where we rented the boat, I was just concerned with quickly putting the fish on ice so we could get back out to continue our walleye fishing. After discovering my catch tipped the scales at 65 pounds and measured 56 1/2 inches, it eventually sunk in just how rare a fish I'd captured!"

Current catch records confirm that the status of our musky fisheries is at a very high level and, in many cases, more big muskies are now being caught than ever before. Two of Wisconsin's most thorough keepers of catch records have been reporting both record numbers and more big muskies being caught during recent years.

The fish that gives musky fishermen everywhere hope that a world record can be attained. An onlooker poses beside Ken O'Brien's 65-pounder from Ontario's Georgian Bay, caught in 1988.

The Vilas County Musky Marathon, which has kept detailed records since 1964, reported not only an all time record 2,237 muskies (78 percent of which were released) were registered into its contest in 1992, but also the capture of the contest's second largest musky ever — 47 pounds 10 ounces. This big musky was not a fluke for Vilas County either, for during the 1994 season, 46 3/4- and 44-pound muskies were registered into the contest.

And, in 1994, the famed Chippewa Flowage reported an all time record 1,596 muskies (90 percent of which were released) were caught as well as an unequaled number of big muskies — 72 muskies weighing 25 pounds or more!

All across Musky Country big muskies have become more common — even 50-pound class muskies showing up in impressive numbers. Here's an honor roll of fish 50 pounds or better caught since 1981: Ken O'Brien, 65 pounds, 1988; Art Barefoot, 59 pounds 11 ounces, 1989; Gene Borucki, 56 pounds 11 ounces, 1984; Gary Ishii, 55 pounds, 1981; Steve Albers, 55 pounds, 1985; Jim Carrol, 54 pounds 3 ounces, 1987; George Quetellin, 52 1/4 pounds, 1994; Don Reed, 51 1/2 pounds, 1982; Dennis Denman, 50 1/2 pounds, 1981; Robert Grutt, 50 1/2 pounds, 1989; John Vaughn, 50 pounds 3 ounces, 1990; Terry Bachman, 50 pounds, 1983; Robert LeMay, 50 pounds, 1983; Ed Barbosa, 58-inch release, 1994; and John Wozny, 57 1/2-inch release, 1994.

Because of the outstanding success of the release program (with 75 to 85 percent of all musky catches now being voluntarily released), there is no serious threat of angler overharvest to most of our fisheries. If there are any threats to the muskellunge and our north country's unspoiled lakes and rivers, they come from potential pollution by man.

These sparkling blue jewels and their finny inhabitants make up Musky Country's most treasured wealth. These riches must be wisely handled, as it is our obligation to pass them on to our children intact.

The recording and preserving of some of muskellunge fishing's greatest angling accomplishments and our sport's rich heritage is what helps perpetuate the great mystique that surrounds this wondrous fish. The common goal of catching the elusive muskellunge, and ultimately one of record class, has lured people from all walks of life — from kings and presidents to just the average Joe. Records are made to be broken and it's only a matter of time before another one of Musky Country's phantom world records makes a brief, but inevitable, appearance and smashes someone's lure. Maybe it will be yours!

THE EVOLUTION OF MUSKY TACKLE

No one can be certain when the first muskellunge was caught. The Native Americans knew of this great fish. Pre-contact copper, bone, stone and shellfish hooks attest to the fact that the Native Americans fished with hook and line. It is uncertain whether any artificial lures with attached hooks were used by these people. Native Americans in the Great Lakes region were known to have used artificial "minnows," made of wood and weighted with lead, to lure fish, including muskies, within range of a spear. References date back to the 1700s.

As white settlers moved into the interior of North America they became aware of the great freshwater fisheries. These settlers brought with them new techniques and technologies — artificial lures, steel hooks and angling methods including the fishing rod and reel. One thing was obvious to the pioneer fisherman, the musky was a special fish that required special tackle.

Row trolling was the method most commonly suited to early muskellunge fishing. The multiplying fishing reels of the mid to late 1800s were very expensive and often a simple handline was used in the early days.

An illustration in Frederick Tolfrey's *Sportsman in Canada*, Volume II, 1845, titled "How to fish for Muskinunge" shows the use of a hand line with a rod — the line neatly coiled on the floor of the boat and controlled in a fashion similar to fly fishing.

Charles Lanman in *A Summer in the Wilderness* (Nyand, Philadelphia, 1847) describes fishing for pike and muskies in the Upper Mississippi with a Mammoth Fly. His 1856 journal, *Adventures in the Wilds of the U.S. and British American Provinces* (Publisher, John W. Moore, Philadelphia, 1856) describes the use of spoon hooks when fishing muskies in the St. Lawrence.

Undoubtedly some of the earlier "reels" used would include the British "Winches" a simple one-to-one ratio reel made of wood and brass. An exciting new development was made by a watchmaker from Kentucky named George Snyder who developed the first multiplying reels around 1812. However, these reels were prohibitively expensive to most anglers of the time. Toward the latter part of the 1800s, the multiplying reels became somewhat more affordable.

In *American Game Fishes*, (Rand McNally, 1892) the essential musky outfit was described:

"The rod should be a good one of split-bamboo, or of ash or lancewood and should weight not more than ten or at the most twelve ounces, and should not exceed nine feet in length. A first-class multiplying reel is indispensable, with seventy five yards of plaited silk line, No. 3, or letter E. The hook should be a Sproat or a O'Shaughnessy, No. 3-0 to 5-0 and tied on a gimp snell. The best bait is a large live minnow, or frog, either for casting or trolling, though for the latter mode of fishing a large trolling spoon with a single hook may be used."

The silk lines used in these days were very strong but required special care. At the end of each day the line had to be wound on a large spool, known as a line dryer, in order to be properly dried to prevent line rot.

Metal lures were the most popular artificial lures used for muskellunge prior to 1900. These included, of course, the spoon which was definitely in use prior to 1850, and the spinner.

Julio Buel is generally credited with being the inventor of the fishing spoon. Legend has it that the "spoon" bait was conceived when Buel dropped a silver dining spoon over the side of his boat only to see fish

A sampling of modern day "metal lures," commonly known as bucktails.

biting at it as it wobbled into the clear depth of Lake Bomoseen, Vermont.

The spoon theory is clearly disproved by Buel's 1852 patent. Julio Buel states in the text of the patent, "I wish it to be clearly understood that I do not claim what is called a spoon, minnow or (common fly), all these have been used before." Buel's patent pictures and clearly describes what would be classified as a "spinner," though at this time they were called trolling spoons.

These spinners were especially deadly on the great muskellunge. These baits were also among the first to be modified to suit the needs of the muskellunge fisherman. It was clear from the start that a special lure was needed. The lure had to be large to whet the appetite of this large predator. It had to be heavy duty to withstand the crushing jaws of the musky.

The St. Lawrence River system — especially the Thousand Islands region — was an early hotbed of muskellunge fishing. Between 1848 and the turn of the century dozens of lure manufacturers showed up on both sides of the border. Chapman, Buehl and Skinner are well known names on spinner and other metal lures of this era. Enterprise Manufacturing Co. (Pflueger) of Akron, Ohio, also had an extensive line of spinners prior to 1900. Other metal lures of note developed over

The "Snodlow" is a rare but effective surface musky plug.

the years include Eppinger's Dardevle Spoon and Johnson's Silver Minnow Spoon.

A couple of lures manufactured in the 1950s and 1960s include Marathon's Musky Houn which was one of the first weighted musky spinners as well as one of the first weight-forward-type spinners. The Musky Houn was an especially deadly lure for the casters of the day. Another important lure was Marathon's Big Slim, one of the first straight shaft bucktails.

Proven musky spinners of today include Mepps, Buchertail, Rizzotail, Eagle Tail, Grim Reaper, etc.

Around the turn of the century lures with attached hooks were being developed. These lures are known as plugs. Generally speaking, there are three types of plugs:

• The floating surface plug attract muskies to strike them on top of the water. These are usually made to imitate an injured fish, frog, mouse or whatever else a musky might want for lunch. An earlier example of this type of plug is the Heddon "300," which was originally developed as a plug for big bass in Florida. Spinners, called "props," were attached to the front and back of this football-shaped piece of wood producing surface commotion, including spray. Another famous early surface plug of this type is the South Bend Surf Oreno. From the 1930s on many surface musky plugs were introduced. Notable examples are the musky version of

Heddon's famous Crazy Crawler, Fred Arbogast's Jitterbug, South Bend's Lunge Oreno and its close relative, the rare musky Surf Oreno, Pflueger's Globe (affectionately known as the Yellow Boy), the Creek Chub Dinger, Injured Minnow and Plunker. Some recent favorites include the Tally Wacker, Frenchy LaMay's Water Thumper, the Hog Wobbler, Swoosh and Hi-Fin's Hawg Buster.

• The floater/diver, now more commonly referred to as "crankbaits." Some of the early examples were developed in the 1910s for use by baitcasting, rather than trolling. Formidable examples of early floater/divers were the musky version Creek Chub Pikie Minnow and Husky Musky. Both of these plugs had a patented (1920) metal lip which forced the plug to dive. South Bend's notorious Bass Oreno

Floater/divers are often referred to as "crankbaits" today. They are usually designed to look like baitfish; in this case, this custom-made bait is painted to resemble a lake trout.

came in a musky size called the Musk Oreno. The diving action on this plug was imparted by a grooved head which forced the plug down when retrieved. Heddon's Musky Vamps came in three sizes. Similar plugs by Shakespeare, Pflueger, Paw Paw and others were not as popular. The Crane Bait, Rapala, DepthRaider and Grandma are fish catchers currently available.

• The sinking plug is the third type of musky plug. The earliest plugs of this type date to the turn of the century. Many of these plugs are referred to as "underwater minnows." They were designed for row trolling rather than baitcasting. Heddon, South Bend, Shakespeare and Pflueger (the earliest) made underwater minnows which had spinners on both ends of a weighted, elongated, round body, which caused these plugs to appear to swim in a straight line when trolled. In recent years, the late Peter Haupt of Hayward, Wisconsin, made a sinking plug called the Ojibway, and it is manufactured in a slightly different form by the Dick Gries Tackle Co. and called the Phantom Ojibway. The Countdown Rapala and Countdown DepthRaider are sinking baits currently in manufacture.

Many lure companies have made musky plugs. Most are derived from or downright copies of the early classics. The exception here is the underwater minnow which essentially disappeared in the 1930s due to its unacceptability to baitcasting.

Old musky plugs are actively sought by collectors.

Some examples are downright rare and expensive. Condition is very important to plug collectors. An old musky plug in new condition in its original box is preferred and in most cases priced at a great premium.

One type of lure that is somewhat unique to musky fishing is the so-called "jerkbaits." The origin of the jerkbait goes back until at least the 19th century. Research into the history and tradition of fish decoys, which are essentially wooden, fish-shaped lures used through the ice in the winter to attract food fish into the range of a spear, has brought information indicating these people used hookless, flat wood lures to attract muskies into open water spearing range. This activity was done both from the shore by throwing the plug out and bringing it back in and by attaching the lure to the front canoe paddle with a line. A musky following the decoy could be reached by the canoe's rear paddler. This was done during the wild rice season (late August/early September). It is interesting to note that at some point in time after contact with white people metal hooks were probably attached. If this happened as long ago as the mid-1800s this type of musky plug would be a candidate for the first wooden plug! Examples of flat, fish-shaped jerk-style baits have turned up some dating back to the early 1900s, if not before then.

One of the first jerkbaits used for muskies in the Boulder Junction, Wisconsin, area lakes is reported to have been carved from basswood by Big Louie St. Germain. "Big Louie" was a famous Chippewa guide. In the 1930s a jerkbait similar to the Lac du Flambeau example was made by a game warden by the name of Frank Long. This was called the Pocahontas. About the same time, the Dean Brothers, Porter of Boulder Junction and Pop of Sayner, were developing jerkbaits of their own design. However, it was Frank Suick of Antigo, Wisconsin, who made the jerkbait famous. His famous Suick's Muskie Thriller is an extremely popular lure even to this day. Frank Suick filed for his patent on March 19, 1947. Frank Suick's feat of 30 legal muskies in 30 days from Pelican Lake

Two extremely popular modern day jerkbaits are the Eddie (middle) and Suick. In the fall, where legal, many musky anglers use these in conjunction with livebait, usually suckers. Note how both baits are painted to resemble a sucker.

in north central Wisconsin put this lure in high demand right from the beginning.

Another jerkbait worthy of note is the Bobbie Bait developed by Robert and Harold VanderVelden of Appleton, Wisconsin. The VanderVelden brothers were janitors at the high-school in town and were able to develop their lures by testing them in the school swimming pool.

Other famous jerkbaits include the Smity, Eddie, Reef Hawg and the Fooler.

Between 1860 and the turn of the century, several companies produced heavy duty reels made for trolling for muskies. Many of these reels were of the large salt water size used primarily for salt water fish. Some of the more important makers were Pflueger, Conroy, Snyder, Edward vomHofe, Hendryx and B.F. Meek's Nos. 4 and 5. Meek was better known for his superb reels called Kentucky Bass reels. They were made of German silver and are highly prized by today's collectors. Perhaps the most important feature of Meek reels was the fact they were multipliers, meaning they reeled

Photos like this help sell musky baits! Bill Crawford, Bob VanderVelden and Ken Ackley with 106 pounds of muskies, caught in July 1956 from the Chippewa Flowage.

in at a faster rate because of the gear ratio.

Around the beginning of the 20th century, the same companies continued to make musky-size reels which were greatly improved and were generally more affordable. It is in the early 1910s period where we see a gradual change from trolling for musky to the more recent technique developed in the South for bass called baitcasting. The William Shakespeare Company of Kalamazoo, Michigan, was one of the first to produce fine baitcasting reels. Pflueger started making some models in the early 1910s and was followed by other famous makers such as the James Heddon Company of Dowagiac, Michigan, and South Bend Bait Company of South Bend, Indiana. They continued making fine musky reels until the onset of World War II in 1941, and returned to making musky reels following the war. Many of the same models were re-introduced in the late 1940s by Pflueger, South Bend and Shakespeare. New models were being developed, but some of the older models were preferred. Pflueger's famous Rocket was highly esteemed in areas such as north central Wisconsin. It could be used for row trolling or baitcasting. Perhaps the Pflueger Supreme was and is an all-time favorite. For many years, from the early 1930s until now, a much favored standard outfit for casting for musky was a Supreme on a Heddon "Pal" rod (hollow metal).

In the mid-1950s, two innovations appeared on the

musky scene. Both were imports. The first was the introduction of the open-faced spinning reel. This method was popular in Europe for many years. At first, spinning seemed strange to American anglers. It was after trying it on game fish found in the United States that fishermen found how versatile and deadly this method could be. The ability to cast light lures long distances was perhaps a feature that didn't lend itself to musky fishing. Muskies and musky fishermen prefer large lures.

When they were introduced, some fishermen tried using the heavier European open-faced and, more recently, closed-faced spinning reels for musky. This type of reel has been refined and improved until the present day. Some musky fishermen seem to prefer the spinning technique. Notable among this type of reel is the Mitchell 300.

The second type of greatly improved musky reels are the high-gear-ratio, free-spooling heavy duty reels with star drags. This type of reel is typified by the famous Ambassadeur series which is a favorite of today's anglers.

The earliest musky rods were made of wood (greenhart and lancewood were preferred materials). Stout rods, four to six feet long, were used for row trolling. This was followed by the use of split bamboo rods which were outstanding in both weight, action and strength. One early famous maker was Leonard. Many early split bamboo musky rods were made by individual crafters to be sold to companies such as Abbey and Imbrie, VL&A, Horrocks-Ibbotson and Montague.

We start to see more use of both solid steel and hollow steel musky rods around the beginning of the 20th century. It wasn't until after World War II when better, more exotic materials were introduced and fast became the choice of musky fishermen, replacing wood and metal. This is because the materials were both light and stronger — solid and hollow fiberglass and all forms of plastic. Musky fishermen are now fortunate to use lightweight rods, often made of graphite.

Anyone interested in research or collecting musky lures, reels, rods, etc. should consider joining the National Fishing Lure Collectors Club. Contact Steve Lumpkin, P.O. Box 0184, Chicago, IL 60690.

To view old musky tackle, visit:
• The National Fresh Water Fishing Hall of Fame, Hayward, Wisconsin, (715) 634-4440.
• The Northland Fishing Museum and Wildlife Gallery, Osseo, Wisconsin, (715) 597-2551.

Musky reels have come a long way. Now, anti-backlash devices make them easier to use and star drags aid in fighting fish.

THE WATERS

Realistically, it is difficult to accurately identify the original range of the musky and the waters it inhabited since records dating to before 1950 are vague at best. On top of this, the musky's range has expanded so much both naturally, as well as artificially (through stocking) that pinpointing origins is very difficult. Some claim that the musky was originally a North American river fish with beginnings in a few larger, select rivers north of the Mason/Dixon Line such as the Mississippi, Wisconsin, St. Lawrence, Niagara, St. Clair, English, French and Ottawa. These river strain muskies are often referred to as the "striped" or "barred" muskies, containing prominent vertical bars. Yet, evidence suggests that another strain of musky existed in the Great Lakes. This unique, pure strain of muskellunge was noticeably different, being spotted like a leopard; thus the nickname "leopard" or spotted musky.

The hybrid, or "tiger," musky has existed for nearly as long as the natural or "true" musky in many of these same environments even though it is now an artificially propagated fish in many southern waters. Before modern day fish management, muskies occasionally mated with northern pike when conditions were right. This phenomena still occurs today naturally in waters all across North America. It is particularly common in shallower, fertile lakes with heavy weed growth and strong pike populations.

What artificial propagation and stocking of hybrids has done is simply expand the range and availability of "tigers," and in some cases the true muskellunge. What was once a rare prize of nature (the tiger) in the original northern ranges, where hybrids are still rarely stocked and appear only by natural happenchance, is now a common occurrence in waters south of the musky's original range, where no natural population existed. These southern musky waters predominantly feature the hybrid, and they are caught regularly — in some situations, they're huge!

The hybrid of these southern waters was initially stocked to provide an additional sport value and serve as a predator for panfish control. The theory was that hybrids were more voracious, less selective feeders than the pure strain of musky, and they grew faster. The combination sounded like the perfect remedy for waters that had an out-of-control panfish base (bluegills, perch, etc.) that needed strong predation. However, in retrospect it is questionable whether this policy actually ever worked in any instance. Interestingly, while the mass introduction of the tiger to all these new waters has created a vast expansion of the musky range, and has provided a great deal of excitement sportfishing-wise, panfish numbers have rarely shown a decrease in these waters nor has the overall size of individual panfish improved.

The range of the natural musky has also expanded through both private club and state-sponsored stocking programs. Muskies of various natural strains now exist in far wider ranges than they did even 15 years ago. States like Illinois, Indiana, Iowa, North Dakota, South Dakota, Missouri and Nebraska, which once had minuscule musky fisheries with state records weighing in the teens, now boast that their musky angling opportunities in some instances rival that of Wisconsin, Minnesota, Michigan, New York, Ohio, Pennsylvania and Ontario. While this is surely arguable, recent state record entries do suggest vastly improved musky fishing opportunities.

Kentucky has a long tradition of great musky fishing at Dale Hollow Lake, the Cave Run Reservoir, and the Green River system.

Illinois' state record for a natural musky jumped from a mere 19 pounds just 10 years ago to 34.3 pounds in 1994. Indiana's state record musky was in the teens less than 10 years ago, and it now stands at 35 1/2 pounds. Iowa has always bragged of a limited but quality musky fishery in its well known water, Lake Okoboji. But now "big fish" has a whole new meaning — Okoboji produced a 40-pound 5-ouncer in 1991. North Dakota brags of a 40-pound hybrid in the record books, but also has an unverified 41-pound natural muskellunge reported in *Musky Hunter* magazine in 1992. Neighboring South Dakota also has a limited overall musky fishery, but can't be discounted in terms of big fish. Its hybrid category officially lists a 33-pounder bagged in 1992, and a 40-pound natural muskellunge brought to the scales in 1991. Missouri's muskellunge fishery, while also limited, can also brag of "big 'uns." Lake of the Ozarks produced a 41-pound 2-ouncer in 1981. And finally, Nebraska didn't even mention muskies a few decades ago, yet now has a 41 1/2-pounder caught in 1992 as its state record! Even the western state of Wyoming is now claiming big muskies. The monstrous Grey Rocks Reservoir gave up a tiger in 1992 that was just shy of 30 pounds (29.37 pounds).

Perhaps the biggest story in newly expanding musky waters has to be the state of Colorado. This southwestern state went from virtually no musky fishery 20 years ago to a state record (tiger) of 19 pounds in 1987. Then it jumped into the front page of the musky world with a 40-pound 2-ounce hybrid in 1994 from Quincy Reservoir, Colorado's now premier musky water. Colorado saw its musky fishery develop almost overnight. The state record tumbled on an annual basis and jumped by leaps and bounds as the fast growing tiger musky really found a new home. Right now there appears to be no end in sight, and the sky's the limit in the hybrid division.

States like Virginia, West Virginia, Kentucky, and Tennessee all had small but apparently original musky fisheries with big fish available. Virginia has several good musky waters, but the New River gave up a 45-pounder in 1989. That's a real "horse" in any water. West Virginia has a fairly strong musky fishery in several of its rivers and reservoirs, and still claims a 43-pounder from the Elk River back in 1955. But its 36.5-pound hybrid, taken in 1994, is the news. Impressive fish indeed.

Kentucky's Dale Hollow Lake has been a long time producer of bigger natural muskies. In fact, it

Tiger muskies have been stocked in many non-traditional musky waters as a way of controlling panfish populations. Being sterile, the species will eventually die out if fisheries officials decide they no longer want them in a body of water.

contains both the spotted and barred fish, which is baffling to both anglers and biologists as to where they originally came from and how they got there. While Dale Hollow doesn't pump out numbers of fish, big ones are surely still there. The state record, however, still stands at 43 pounds — taken from Dale Hollow in 1978. Cave Run Reservoir and the Green River system have pumped out a bunch of quality muskies in the past decade — several in the 30-pound-plus range, and a few over 40. These waters are considered the best prospects by locals.

Nearby Tennessee has also produced its share of lunkers within a limited overall fishery. In 1983, Norris Reservoir gave up a 42 1/2-pounder. It's interesting to note that the musky enthusiasts of Tennessee also lay claim to the Dale Hollow record.

Still, the more traditional, well-known musky waters of the north, such as Wisconsin, Michigan, Minnesota, New York, Ohio, Pennsylvania and the Canadian province of Ontario continue to produce the biggest fish and the largest selection of waters. Even in these traditional musky producers the musky

Reservoirs, known as flowages in the northern range of Musky Country, can offer outstanding fishing. Wisconsin's Chippewa Flowage yielded the world record 69-pound 11-ounce musky by Louis Spray in 1949.

ranges have been expanded by artificial propagation of both natural and hybrid muskies. In almost every case, this expansion of natural musky range in traditional areas has really had an impact on waters in the southern portions of these states; particularly in close proximity to big cities. Both hybrids and naturals have been stocked successfully in many waters.

Speaking of traditional waters, the strength in all these ranges is diversity as well as population. While smaller musky fisheries in southern waters are usually limited to large reservoirs and their connecting riverways, traditional regions such as Wisconsin boast of muskies in a wide variety of lakes, rivers, flowages, reservoirs, creeks and even ponds. There are so many waters with muskies in these parts that there are, honestly, too many to mention each by name. Everything from shallow, coffee-stained flowages and rivers, to deep, clear cold natural lakes can and usually do hold solid populations of muskellunge. Trophy potential can vary greatly on these various waters, as well as overall population per acre, but viable musky fisheries of all kinds exist.

The most waters in Wisconsin containing muskies are located in Vilas, Oneida and Sawyer counties. Lakes, rivers and flowages inside these counties have, in fact, accounted for the state's biggest and most fish annually. Sawyer County is

unique historically since it is one of the few places in the world that has produced bona fide, documented 60-pound-plus muskies. The current world record of 69 pounds 11 ounces, a 63-incher caught by Louis Spray, came from Sawyer County's most famous water — the Chippewa Flowage. "The Chip" is actually a large, stained water reservoir and part of the original Chippewa River system.

However, right down the road is Lac Courte Oreilles — a large, deep, clear natural lake that produced another 60-pound-plus fish that was also a world record — 67 1/2 pounds, a 60 1/4-incher, caught by longtime outdoor writer Cal Johnson. These angling feats are especially unique when you consider that no other county throughout the diverse musky state of Wisconsin has ever produced a musky weighing anywhere near 60 pounds. Both of these "super hawgs" were taken only three months apart in 1949 — what a year that must have been! Lac Courte Oreilles, by the way, can also lay claim to being one of the few waters to produce more than one over 60 pounds. Louis Spray's 61-pound 13-ouncer, caught in 1940, was yet another well documented 60-pounder taken from this special lake. Why this body of water produced fish of a size caliber so far larger than anything recorded anywhere else in the state is still somewhat baffling. What's even more unusual is that Lac Courte Oreilles as well as "The Chip" have never produced another musky since the 1940s that even remotely approaches the stature of these three fish.

In fact, by today's records and standards on any annual comparison, Sawyer County waters don't stack up to be any better than the multitude of musky waters scattered throughout the rest of the state. Vilas, Oneida and Iron counties (northeastern Wisconsin), actually have more overall musky fisheries, and produce just as many numbers as well as giant fish on any given year. In almost every case, the top-end fish is in the low to mid 40-pound range. Outstanding fish in every respect, but not even close to the historic 60-pound benchmark.

Wisconsin's big sleeper on the horizon appears to be the series of larger reservoirs in the central part of the state that string along the Wisconsin River. These waters, unknown as musky fisheries in books of the past, have received nearly two decades of strong stocking to supplement once-limited trophy fisheries. Today it is not uncommon to hear of a 40-pounder coming from Lake DuBay, Lake Wausau, Mohawksin, Half Moon, Petenwell, Castle Rock or Lake Wisconsin, all flowages of this Wisconsin River system in central Wisconsin. Muskies near the 50-pound barrier have already come from both this stretch of river and its reservoirs. Don't be surprised to read about a super lunker from any of these waters in the near future.

However, never underestimate the low-population musky fisheries that also exist across Wisconsin. Niche spots such as Lake Butte des Mortes, near Oshkosh, occasionally pop up with huge muskies well exceeding 40 pounds. So does the giant Lake Winnebago. The fertile Madison Chain of lakes (Mendota, Monona, Wingra, etc.) is also worth a mention. Both tigers and trues are now commonplace to these waters in the mid 20-pound range.

Minnesota has also provided a strong historical musky fishery, though it is often overshadowed by its neighbor, Wisconsin. Minnesota's musky range has been expanded greatly by new stockings. Traditional favorites such as Leech Lake (near Walker) are every bit as good today as ever. But the thought of muskies roaming huge Mill Lacs and Winnibigoshish, which were once void of muskellunge, is enough to excite any musky angler or researcher. Mille Lacs' relatively new musky introduction effort is showing signs of eruption. Twenty-pounders are common. They're also fast growing and very healthy. Thirty-pounders are just around the corner. With the fantastic forage base in these sprawling, shallow waters, who knows what the future offers?

The Little Boy Chain, north of Brainerd, is still a strong musky producer and is often regarded as Minnesota's best-kept musky secret. It has both solid numbers and bigger fish in the 35-pound class. The small lakes surrounding the big metropolis of Minneapolis might be the biggest musky surprise of all, however. Tigers in the 20- to 30-pound range are present in surprisingly strong numbers. Shore anglers are catching them regularly, and swimmers have developed an almost "Jaws-like" respect for them after several reported incidents of leg bite attacks.

Minnesota's most underrated, but highest potential water for trophy muskies might be the Mississippi River stretch near Grand Rapids. The overall numbers are somewhat low, but the size potential is top notch. Mid 40-pound class fish are caught often enough by the limited fishing pressure to suggest there's something there worth checking. The Big and Little Fork Rivers also have good musky potential. Both rivers have fairly strong populations along with an occasional lunker pushing the 30-pound mark.

The state of Michigan is worth a discussion all its own. Both the lower state and the Upper Peninsula have some great musky waters, yet for the most part they go unnoticed with the exception of Lake St. Clair. This giant of a lake racked up some legendary musky catches in the 1950s, and then plummeted as a musky producer for over 20 years afterward. Pollution and overexploitation were just two of many culprits thought to have caused this demise. The good news is Lake St. Clair has since made a great comeback. The predominant Great Lakes musky is now making an impressive return although fish over 35 pounds are still noticeably absent.

Other Michigan waters worth a check are Indian, Stanley, Chicagoan, Thousand Island, and Brevort in the Upper Peninsula, and Bankson in the southern state. None of these lakes have populations that rival a typical Wisconsin water, but they surely have some big fish.

Ohio and Pennsylvania have also made their mark in musky history books with fish exceeding 50 pounds, but their overall scope of musky fishing opportunities is far more limited. This doesn't diminish the potential that exists on the waters that do have muskies. Pymatuning Reservoir in Pennsylvania was the hottest musky water in the country back in the mid 1970s, but has since really slacked off. However, Raystown Reservoir and the Allegheny Reservoir have produced some recent fish of top end stature (over 40 pounds). So has the Allegheny River and the Susquehanna River.

Piedmont Lake in Ohio has made its mark with the state record of 55 pounds 2 ounces. But nearby West Branch and Milton reservoirs have produced more recent outsized catches of muskies weighing 45 pounds or more; with West Branch producing several throughout the past decade.

New York is wrapped in musky controversy because of the disqualification of all the Lawton and Hartman catches. Research along with taped confessions of Len Hartman have cast doubt on the real potential of New York's many fine musky waters. It now appears that the St. Lawrence River system, once thought to have produced more 50- and 60-pound class muskies than all other waters combined, never actually produced any! This great waterway was surely one of the best producers ever of 50-inch class muskies, but it now appears obvious that it was not the monster water it was claimed to be.

Regardless, the St. Lawrence has continued to produce 50-inch muskies. Other top waters in the Empire State include Lake Chautauqua and the Upper Niagara River.

Finally, while Lake of the Woods is usually considered Canadian water, Minnesota definitely can lay claim to part of it as well as its awesome musky potential and history. This giant piece of God's Country just might be the best overall musky water in the world. Great numbers, great size and great management all add up to great musky potential. Lake of the Woods has it all. This is also anoth-

er example of a fishery that has withstood the tests of time, and now appears to be getting even better. Strong catch and release practices coupled with a 52-inch size limit have made "The Woods" superb in nearly every category.

Lake of the Woods, of course, is also part of Ontario; a massive southern Canadian province. Arguably, Ontario's musky waters are unequalled at this point in terms of trophy potential. While the entire musky management philosophy in Canada does not include any artificial stockings, Ontario remains a dominating force in big musky catches. Perhaps this in itself is its biggest asset. Strong native populations of muskies, untampered by competition with exotics, could be a reason for the impressive average size of the fish caught. However, water size is also a factor. In general, most of the lakes in Ontario are far larger than most of

Sundown near Coleman's Reef in Ontario's famed Eagle Lake.

the natural lakes and flowages in the United States. For example, the legendary Lac Courte Oreilles of Wisconsin, producer of two 60-pounders, is considered a big lake at just over 5,000 acres. That's nothing more than a good sized bay in Lake of the Woods, Eagle Lake or Georgian Bay.

Here is where the "gold fish bowl" theory seems to have some credibility. This simply means — the bigger the bowl, the bigger the fish will grow. In addition, put a few fish in a big bowl and they grow big. Load that same bowl up with lots of fish, and their growth is stunted. In common sense terms, the larger lake principle simply makes a big musky less accessible, just like a big whitetail buck is more likely to survive in a huge wilderness forest than in habitats that feature small woodlots.

With that in mind, history has been favorable to famous Ontario waters like Lake of the Woods, Rainy Lake, Eagle Lake, Lac Seul, the French River and Georgian Bay. Collectively, these well known musky waters produce more 50-inch class muskies than any other group of waters in North America. Each has had its peak in producing record class fish in numbers, and they still give them up with regularity.

Lake of the Woods has produced some record class fish in the past and continues to give up its share of 50-inchers. Eagle Lake has produced two of the few muskies in history that legitimately broke the

60-pound benchmark. And the more recently discovered Lac Seul waterway, known mostly in the past for its walleye and pike potential, is now protected by a total catch and release regulation. Lake Wabigoon, near Dryden, was sizzling hot in the late 1970s; it produced countless 40- to 50-pound range muskies only to see a major dropoff in the mid 1980s. A strict 52-inch size limit has now encouraged a comeback. The real story of big muskies throughout the late 1980s was Georgian Bay; a large section of Lake Huron. Several areas inside of Georgian Bay, including the Moon River basin, the lower French River, and various channels and canals, have turned out some incredible world class fish including muskies just shy of the 60-pound mark. The potential for a record will always exist there by sheer size of this entire piece of water alone. Its 350 miles of shoreline virtually guarantee that a few 'lunges will survive to that eye-popping size.

However, smaller, less traveled waters throughout Ontario that have limited road travel, or are still considered fly-in trips, contain some incredible potential. Some good selections here would include: Minnaki, Dryberry, Rowan, Pipestone, Dog Paw, Cavier, Thadeus, and portions of the Winnipeg River. Other less known waters are sure to exist and surface at anytime.

The real Canadian sleeper is the Montreal area right now; specifically the Ottawa River system. Virtually unknown up to this writing, the Ottawa River has quietly produced more muskies over 50 pounds in the early 1990s than any other place in the world. Ed Barbosa's 58-inch world record release in the fall of 1994 tops an ever increasing list of lunkers. These Ottawa River muskies are big fish with great length, thick girths, and a solid, healthy look. Why the Ottawa River has suddenly come onto the musky scene with these giants, and where they were beforehand, remains a question unanswered. Perhaps it's nothing more than an oversight. But the bottom line is — the big fish are there in numbers. In fact, the Ottawa River is quite possibly the best place left on the planet to bag a world record. It ranks right up there with Georgian Bay. Who knows how long this will last. The only hope is that today's release minded angler will continue to set standards even higher as they fish this unexploited trophy fishery.

The real story about the traditionally known waters is that, for the most part, they seem to be getting better. A strong population combined with aggressive stocking efforts in many of these historic locales suggests a continuation of this tradition. Perhaps the biggest debt of gratitude in all waters mentioned may go to the musky angler himself. The staunch catch and release policy practiced by the vast majority of today's serious musky hunters has had many unforeseen positive results for fish managers. In fact, in many cases, stocking is no longer necessary. No longer are numbers of muskies under 50 inches harvested for the taxidermist or the table. They're released to fight another day.

The biggest surprise of all to fish managers across the continent is the catch and release attitude toward big, trophy class muskies of 50 inches or more. Each season more anglers are subscribing to an almost religious catch and release cult of the largest of muskies. Education has had a great deal to do with this, as well as the development of the replica taxidermy business. Anglers now realize more than ever that the 50-incher is the most precious resource of all; and that he or she can indeed "have their cake and eat it too" now that replica taxidermy can virtually duplicate the length, girth and coloring of the catch. The most recent comeback of consistent catches of mid 50-inchers weighing in the upper 40-pound class is a telltale signal that the future looks bright for freshwater's most heralded prize.

THE MUSKY
CLUB EQUATION

On the surface, the very existence of musky clubs appears to be a contradiction in terms. It's puzzling, even downright paradoxical. Given the nature of the fish and of the men and women in its thrall, the musky club seems about as (un)likely as an association of bounty hunters or wolf trappers. The musky fisherman is, after all, as solitary a creature as the elusive, magnificent prize he pursues. And if he is not feared, exactly, his extreme intensity tends to make "normal" folks — those unafflicted by musky fever — a little uncomfortable.

The musky fisherman's commitment is total; his dedication, complete. Driven by a desire that often teeters on the brink of obsession, he tracks this greatest of freshwater trophies relentlessly, from the first soft days of spring through the blazing midsummer heat to the bone-chilling cold at the dark end of autumn. The musky is as much an idea — an embodiment of qualities that add up to something uniquely challenging — as it is a fish, and in the realm of the mind time has no particular relevance. It could be an hour since the last hook-up — but it could just as well be a year. It makes no difference to the true musky fisherman, because each cast, the first and the thousandth and every one after that, is made in the utter conviction that it will be *the* cast. And if the bucktail or the crankbait or the jerkbait returns unscathed from its dangerous mission, the musky angler, to his eternally optimistic way of thinking, is one cast closer to his next fish.

Virtually by definition, the musky fisherman is a fanatic, a loner who moves at the shadowy fringe of polite society. If he weren't chasing muskies, he'd be immersed in some equally arcane and rigorous avocation; flying hybrid falcons at prairie grouse, for example, or running field trial dogs from horseback, or bowhunting (with a longbow, not a compound) for bighorn sheep. In short, the person who fishes for 'lunge — independent, self-motivated, a hater of crowds — is perhaps the last individual you'd expect to join a club. As they say in law enforcement, he doesn't fit the profile.

How, then, do you explain the musky club phenomenon? Well, you can argue that the musky fisherman — again, like the fish itself — is an unpredictable beast who delights in confounding expectations out of sheer, unbridled orneriness. But the truth of the matter is that even fanatics tend eventually to sniff one another out, and that, at a basic level, every

Members of a musky club brave a morning fog as they await the beginning of a club outing.
Preceding pages — A scene from the National Championship Musky Open, held annually in Eagle River, Wisconsin. Co-sponsored by the Wisconsin Musky Clubs Alliance and the Eagle River Chamber of Commerce, it is the largest tournament of its kind.

species craves a certain amount of contact with its kind. The musky hunter can hardly expect to strike up a meaningful conversation on his favorite topic with, say, the sullen taxpayer occupying the next stool at the lunch counter. The average Joe simply doesn't walk the walk or talk the talk. By joining a club (or forming one), the musky fisherman can, at the very least, enjoy the company of kindred spirits. He can (guardedly) compare notes on tackle and techniques, share war stories about monumental battles, discuss such storied destination as the Thousand Islands, Georgian Bay and Lake of the Woods. He probably won't divulge any real secrets, though. As the veteran musky angler said of the brash young upstart, "I taught him everything he knows — but I didn't teach him everything I know."

In addition to holding regular meetings and a gala annual banquet, most clubs organize several fishing outings every year to some renowned body of water like the Chippewa Flowage or the Eagle River Chain. The competition is intense but friendly; little different, really, from the traditional "first, biggest, and most" wagering done by any group of sportsman on an away-from-home adventure. The same spirit characterizes the season-long intra-club contests that have long been a fixture on the musky fishing scene. Nothing more is at stake than bragging rights — but there are always members who take bragging rights very, very seriously.

Camaraderie and common interest are, to be sure, important factors in the musky club equation. But the typical club today embraces loftier aspirations. Education and advocacy are the watchwords; boil down the laundry list of objectives found in any club's charter, and you end up with this — a fierce, uncompromising devotion to improving the muskellunge fishery. There is no better evidence of this than the fact that musky clubs took the lead in promoting catch and release, long before it was fashionable to do so.

It is not overstating the case to say that catch and release is the single most beneficial practice ever to come down the pike (so to speak), or that it has literally been the salvation of the musky fishery in waters subject to heavy angling pressure. The legendary Lee Wulff's dictum that "a great gamefish is too valuable to be caught only once" applies doubly to a trophy musky, which because of its rarity, longevity, and position at the very pinnacle of the food chain, takes years to replace after it is removed from the ecosystem.

Regardless, the lion's (musky's?) share of the credit for the widespread acceptance of the catch and release ethic has to go to the many musky clubs that continue to work tirelessly to promote it. The effectiveness of this campaign to change the way anglers think is undisputable; for example, it was not that long ago that the clients of famed Eagle River guide George Langley kept far more muskies than they released. In recent years, however, Langley's been able to count the number of fish boated and kept by his clients on the fingers of one meaty hand. And his experience is the rule, not the exception. Musky anglers everywhere have taken to catch and release with the zeal of converts to a new religion.

If this were the only accomplishment that American and Canadian musky clubs could point to, it would be more than enough. But they have been active on many other fronts as well. Musky clubs enjoy a long history of stocking fish, both to supplement or restore native populations and to establish the species in areas where it was not originally present. Indeed, what has grown to become the largest musky organization in the world, Muskies, Inc., was founded for the specific purpose of expanding musky fishing opportunities in the state of Minnesota.

Musky clubs have also demonstrated their ability to be a force in the political arena, lobbying not only for biologically-sound fishing regulations, but for stringent anti-pollution laws and for measures to prevent degradation of habitat. Some organizations have even stepped in where angels fear to tread, and taken a stand on the controversial issue of native fishing rights. Always, the welfare of the resource is the bottom line.

Financial support for muskellunge research is another part of the formula. From such fundamental work as creel censusing to advanced radio-telemetry tracking projects, musky clubs have contributed more than their fair share of dollars (not to mention legwork). Fishing logs and other data recorded by club members also help biologists to better understand the habits and behaviors of this mysterious freshwater predator.

The range of activities in which musky clubs participate is a match for the range of the fish itself. Many clubs feature "Take a Kid Fishing" days, others organize outings for disabled anglers. They hold open-to-the-public fishing seminars, run booths at sportsmen's shows to spread the catch and release gospel, sponsor fund-raising tournaments, cooperate with state fisheries agencies on stocking and habitat improvement projects ... the list goes on. Make no mistake: the members of musky clubs work hard and diligently, volunteering countless hours of labor for no tangible reward, just the satisfaction of knowing that they've made a difference — and there's no doubt whatsoever that musky clubs have made a difference. If musky fishing is more popular than ever (according to the tackle manufacturers, anyway), it's because there are more muskies in more places than ever before. It's a gratifying turn of events, one that

musky clubs should take great pride in. It could not have happened without them.

The history of musky clubs begins where you would expect it to: Wisconsin, where the muskellunge is the state fish, and the canons and the traditions of the sport run deep. The musky is part of the cultural fabric of the northern lake country; it's said that the musky — or, more accurately, the money spent by the legions of anglers who pursue it — is what built the schools. So it's not at all surprising that the Muskellunge Club of Wisconsin, founded in 1953, is the most venerable musky club in the nation. To illustrate its antiquity, one of the club's first orders of business was fighting to ban the long-accepted practice of shooting muskies to subdue them once they were hauled near

How times have changed. It was 1976 when members of Bill's Musky Club of Wausau, Wisconsin, held an outing of the Eagle River Chain, with Andy Anderson (kneeling) taking first place, Paul Austin (standing, left) placing second and Steve Stroyny taking third. Today, the club still holds outings, but the photos that would result would feature anglers releasing their muskies rather than keeping them. Musky clubs like Bill's have been at the forefront of promoting catch and release.

the boat. (Of course, many a writhing musky was shot after it was already in the boat — and many a musky angler took an unplanned swim as the result of errant aim, or because he employed a load that was just a hair too potent for the task.)

But the issue that truly galvanized the Muskellunge Club of Wisconsin — and which continues to polarize the musky fishing community — was motor trolling. Accepted without question elsewhere in the United States and Canada as a legitimate method, motor trolling hal been resolutely opposed by Wisconsin musky anglers as unsporting; the equivalent, they argue, of ground-swatting a covey of quail or potting a grouse on a tree limb. Whether any good biological reason exists for opposing motor trolling is doubtful, especially in this age of catch and release. Nevertheless, the Muskellunge Club of Wisconsin has been at the forefront in the ongoing battle over legalizing motor trolling on the state's designated musky waters.

And just as Wisconsin boasts the nation's oldest musky club, so does it claim to what is probably the largest independent musky group in the country. Founded by the late Bill Hoeft of Wausau, Wisconsin, in 1964, the aptly named Bill's Musky Club had, at one time, some 1,100 members. Today, over 600 still swell the rolls. It was Bill Hoeft's dream that a member of his club would one day land an all-tackle world record from Wisconsin waters, and thereby bring the record back to the state where he thought it belonged. Although Hoeft lived to see the record return to Wisconsin, it didn't happen in quite the way he envisioned — instead of a new record being established, the old record, Louis Spray's 69-pound, 11-ounce Chippewa Flowage fish caught in 1949, was restored when the 1957 "Lawton Musky" was, in 1992, declared a hoax.

Most of the members of Bill's Musky Club hail from north-central Wisconsin, but there is a smattering of dues-payers from as far away as California. And Bill's is one of the 18 clubs that comprise the Musky Alliance of Wisconsin. Representing approximately 2,000 sportsmen, the Alliance co-sponsors, with the Eagle River Chamber of Commerce, an annual three-day tournament that may well be the largest event of its kind. More than 800 anglers participate in the annual renewal. The proceeds are earmarked to offset the operating costs of cooperatively managed hatcheries in Wausau, Portage, and Wild Rose. (The Wild Rose hatchery produces the spotted, Great Lakes-strain muskellunge, which is currently being re-introduced to its historical range in the waters of Green Bay.) The Alliance is unique in that its member clubs are a mixture of "independents" and chapters of Muskies, Inc., the national "umbrella" organization. Without wanting to belabor the

point, many Wisconsin clubs have chosen to not affiliate themselves with Muskies, Inc., because of that group's neutral stance on motor trolling.

The colorful saga of Muskies, Inc., could fill an entire book. And, in fact, it has: *History of Muskies, Inc.: The First Twenty-Six Years of Progress*, by Kermit Benson (1993). Muskies, Inc., began when the late Gil Hamm, an affable, persuasive contractor from St. Paul, got hooked on musky fishing in the mid-1960s. The fish even invaded his dreams — "I fell out of bed twice trying to land big muskies," he recalled. To Hamm's way of thinking, there was no reason in the world for Minnesota, the state of 10,000 lakes, to have only 100 designated for muskies — especially when neighboring Wisconsin boasted some 700 recognized musky waters.

Muskies, Inc., was born in 1966 of Hamm's dissatisfaction with the status quo. The group got down to brass tacks in a hurry. A $30,000 "musky appropriation" from the Minnesota legislature in 1967 was its first major victory, and hinted at many more to come. Its inaugural fund-raising tournament was held in 1968, the same year that Muskies, Inc., began

Musky clubs were the earliest promoters of catch and release. Now the ethic is spilling over to anglers who pursue other species as a way of ensuring the future of their sport.

promoting the then-radical idea that would ultimately revolutionize musky fishing — catch and release. In 1971, the first satellite chapter was organized in Fargo, North Dakota; chapters in Illinois and Missouri followed suit in 1975. With the addition of an astonishing 14 new chapters spanning the length and breadth of musky country in 1978, Muskies, Inc., firmly established itself as the national voice of the musky angler — and as the musky's best friend whenever and wherever decisions affecting its welfare were being contemplated.

Today, with some 40 chapters and roughly 6,000 members, Muskies, Inc., remains squarely in the musky movement. Well over a quarter-million muskies have been stocked by MI chapters; millions in cash and in-kind contributions have been applied to musky management, research, education, and advocacy. But the most significant achievement of this fine organization, the propagation of the catch and release ethic (you might call MI the Johnny Appleseed of catch and release), is the hardest to quantify. An analysis done in 1990 concluded that nearly 47,000 muskies had been released by MI members alone since 1967. Assuming a 70 percent survival rate, the value of these fish to the economy was estimated to be in excess of $4 million! And there is no telling how many tens of thousands of muskies have been released by non-members whose "conversion" from catch and keep was at least partially attributable to the Muskies, Inc., campaign.

The official purposes of Muskies, Inc., are, with minor variations, a blueprint common to musky clubs across the continent:

• To promote a high quality muskellunge fishery.

• To support selected conservation practices based on scientific merit and carried out by authorized federal and state agencies.

• To promote muskellunge research.

• To establish hatcheries and rearing ponds and introduce the species into suitable waters.

• To support the abatement of water pollution.

• To maintain records of habits, growth, and range of species.

• To disseminate muskellunge information.

• To promote good fellowship and sportsmanship among men, women, and children.

These are essentially the same purposes as those stated in the charter of Muskies Canada, the exception being that stocking is not yet an important part of the musky scene north of the border. Bruce Parks of Toronto is credited with founding Muskies Canada in 1978; the group presently includes six chapters and approximately 400 members. Although the Canadian chapters of Muskies, Inc., all "defected" to Muskies Canada shortly after its formation, the two national organizations maintain a close and cordial working relationship. Recently, they've both been deeply involved in efforts to protect the musky fishery on Ontario's sprawling Lac Seul, where exploitation of a relatively unsophisticated population of muskies by catch and keep anglers forced the provincial Ministry of Natural Resources to impose emergency release-only regulations.

If anything, Muskies Canada stresses catch and release even more emphatically than does its American counterpart. Its publication is entitled *The Release Journal,* and instead of using words like "tournament" or "derby" it refers to its contests as "Live Release Outings." All muskies caught at these affairs are released; the honor system is used to determine the winners. You get the feeling that any Muskies Canada member with the temerity to actually keep a 'lunge is doomed to be regarded by his peers as a despicable lout.

The reason that musky clubs have been so remarkably successful in accomplishing their diverse goals is simple: because members bring the same level of enthusiasm, energy, and dedication to club activities as they do to their single-minded pursuit of *Esox masquinongy.* Largely due to their efforts, the future of musky fishing has never looked brighter.

EPILOGUE:
FAIR CHASE? FAIR GAME?

When my brother catches a trout he wants to keep, he sticks a thumb down the fish's mouth and places his forefinger across the back of its head. With a quick snap of his wrist he'll break the trout's back.

"That way they don't die anguishing in my fishing vest," he chides me.

When I hook a trout I'd like to keep it simply goes into my vest or a creel. Death by asphyxiation, I figure, is less painful than the seemingly traumatic measure Tom uses. Besides, I can't bring myself to do that.

My brother and I are each comfortable with our manner of dispatching the few trout we do keep, but catch and release advocates look down on us for keeping and eating any fish.

Tom and I fly fish for trout, though fly fishing purists who only cast dry flies would snub us — because we also use nymphs and streamers. In turn, we both consider anglers who use spinners or bait for trout "meat fishermen." But then, some non-anglers believe it's not ethical to fish at all.

When we fish muskies, a friend and I are less alike in our views of "proper" behavior. He will only cast for fish. "It's the only sporting way to fish artificials," he claims. Where legal and in lakes where casting isn't a practical method of catching them, I've trolled for muskies. In fall, he soaks suckers on traditional single-hook lines; I use quick-strike rigs, believing I can more easily and safely release muskies taken on them.

The ethics of angling, of course, be it for trout, muskies or any other fish, are personal. No two people share the same standards. Nor do personal standards remain rigid — over time, an individual's viewpoints and conduct change, and yesterday's troller may become strictly a "plug flinger," or vice versa.

Beyond the personal ethic, there is also a societal or cultural dynamic to how we view and deal with muskies and other resources. In the late 19th and early 20th centuries, for instance, commercial fishermen in the Great Lakes states, Ontario and Quebec harvested thousands of pounds of muskies every year. After the species was protected from commercial harvest, fishermen in some areas considered muskies a nuisance, a trash fish. Like lake sturgeon, muskies devastated fine cotton twine nets set for smaller, salable fish. And, when captured by disgruntled commercial fishers, muskies and sturgeon were brought to shore and stacked like cordwood, to rot beneath the sultry summer sun.

Early non-commercial anglers were no less culpable when it came to what we now consider shabby treatment of the species. Muskies were speared, dynamited and seined. When caught on hook and line, the fish were usually clubbed or shot at boatside or kept alive until weighed, then killed for food or photography, or to have their heads varnished as ornaments nailed to cabin walls. Muskies were seldom released, at least alive.

During their day, only 40 years ago in some instances, these customs were regarded normal and proper. Today, we consider the practices unethical at best, illegal at worst. We hold the musky in esteem, consider it a trophy fish. And this begs the question: Why in only a few decades have we so radically changed our attitude toward the musky resource?

Undoubtedly because that resource, in response to past and increased pressures humankind has placed upon it, has greatly, perhaps exponentially, diminished. Our past indifferences to the well-being of muskies and other fish populations are now exacerbated by increased angling pressure, habitat loss and water quality degradation.

Angling pressure on muskies has increased dramatically in the last two decades, and that pressure has come in several forms. First, the serious musky angler has evolved to a target-fish specialist, well-educated and well-equipped to catch the species. The ranks of these anglers have grown, too, and they appreciate more free time and increased access to waters containing muskies than their predecessors did a generation ago. These specialists' uses of sonar and other modern fishing electronics, new lines, lures and other improved equipment, and their ability to easily move from lake to lake on hard-topped roads and concrete boat ramps — technology and mobility old-time fishing guides scoff at as substitutes for patience and hard-gained, time-on-the-water experience — means more fish, especially large muskies, see vastly increased angler pursuit. Fisheries managers, unlike yesterday's sand-trail-rowboat guides, are more concerned about the rising strain placed on the musky resource, especially the lost genetic dowry of the largest individuals of its populations, the preferred harvest goals of today's trophy musky anglers.

Habitat loss and water quality degradation are concerns of anglers and resource professionals alike. Water pollution has certainly diminished the traditional range of muskies in some regions, and, even in areas untouched by industrial development, airborne pollutants and byproduct contamination from natural hydrologic cycling — acid rain, atmospheric pesticide aerosols and endemic mercury circulation — are creating increasing anxiety over the health of present and future musky fisheries.

As the human population continues to grow, so does its lust for life near water, and unchecked shoreline development and the consequent degradation of musky feeding and spawning areas follows. Avaricious real estate developers, disinterested zoning authorities, jet skiers, cigarette boat enthusiasts and even riparian non-anglers whose fertilizers and lawn clippings find their way into musky waters must share the blame for this debasement of habitat.

To a certain extent, our increased sensitivity to the fragility of the musky resource has prompted us to actions to conserve it. In the last 40 to 50 years, musky research, cultivation expertise and management techniques have advanced greatly. We have extended, through hatchery culturing and stocking, musky populations in waters where they never occurred in nature. Through the same processes, we have maintained harvestable populations in waters historically fished by musky anglers. And through harvest regulation we have sustained, to a lesser degree, indigenous populations of fish, or at least segments of those populations, in their native waters.

It is fortunate that musky anglers today, however successful they are at catching fish, have become increasingly conservation-minded. Angler organizations have been particularly responsible for teaching and forwarding the practice of catch and release. Club efforts have helped sustain musky stocking and fisheries research, and have imbued the fishing public with a greater concern for the future of all warm water fisheries, not only those of muskies.

Even now in our so-called "age of environmental enlightenment," however, we must look deeper into the consequences of our musky management and fishing practices. Is it ecologically ethical, for instance, for us to continue to introduce the species in waters where it never existed? (Surely, after more than a century of introductions of exotic trout species, primarily German brown trout, in native brook trout waters, the argument over the propriety of those stockings and their potential damage to native fish populations remains pervasive.)

Also, through intensified hatchery raising of muskies, how are we affecting the genetic integrity of the species? Will the fishery slowly evolve to a put-and-take angling proposition, supplanting genetically superior native strains of muskies with less well adapted, more easily caught and less vigorous artificial strains? Indeed, will the "musky mystique" endure if and when we know our jerkbaits and bucktails are aimed principally at congenitally restrained, hatchery-raised end products?

And how will we be judged, a generation from now, as expediters of fishing tournaments and as wall-mount-trophy-seekers? ... as members of a culture that tolerated overexploitation of resources and allowed fisheries and other wildlife habitat to decay and dwindle in the name of progress?

In any discussion of ethics, as is the usual case, we raise more questions than we answer. But this is how ethical thought evolves. Even the seemingly minor investigation of thought that initiated this dialogue — how an angler should treat fish he has caught — has no simple, generally accepted answer. As anglers we have to deal with those quandaries on a personal basis. But this is how ethical thought becomes practice.

From a holistic, societal perspective, it is perhaps more immediately important — and on this we will be judged by future generations — that our collective ethical behavior go beyond differences of opinion on how we treat individual fish or even individual species, so that it also serves to perpetuate the integrity of whole ecological systems that muskies, walleyes, loons, ducks and other creatures, including ourselves, must share.

The final analysis of our conduct, individually and as a culture, no doubt, will consider how narrowly or broadly, how selfishly as user groups or how magnanimously — despite our consumptive inevitabilities — as good stewards we viewed, protected and used, our natural endowments.